week

Campaign
for President

Campaign for President

The Managers Look at '76

Edited by
Jonathan Moore
Janet Fraser

A Project of the Institute of Politics,
John Fitzgerald Kennedy School of Government,
Harvard University

Ballinger Publishing Company • **Cambridge, Massachusetts**
A Subsidiary of J.B. Lippincott Company

International Standard Book Number: 0-88410-664-0

Library of Congress Catalog Card Number: 77-12033

Printed in the United States of America

Library of Congress Cataloging in Publication Data

Main entry under title:

Campaign for President.

Proceedings of a conference held in Cambridge, Mass., Dec. 3-5, 1976, and sponsored by the Institute of Politics of Kennedy School of Government.

Includes index.
1. Presidents—United States—Election—1976— Congresses. 2. United States—Politics and government—1974-1977—Congresses. I. Moore, Jonathan. II. Fraser, Janet. III. Kennedy School of Government. Institute of Politics.
E868.C35   329'.023'730925   77-12033
ISBN 0-88410-664-0

Contents

The Authors

The authors were participants in the conference on 1976 presidential campaign decisionmaking held in Cambridge, Massachusetts, from December 3 through 5, 1976, sponsored by the Institute of Politics in the John Fitzgerald Kennedy School of Government, Harvard University.

DAVID S. BRODER, associate editor of the *Washington Post*
BENJAMIN D. BROWN, deputy campaign director for Governor Jimmy Carter
PATRICK H. CADDELL, pollster for Governor Jimmy Carter
PETER P. CURTIN, political director for Senator Frank Church
JOHN D. DEARDOURFF, media consultant for President Gerald R. Ford
MICHAEL RAOUL-DUVAL, special counsel to President Gerald R. Ford
JAMES M. FRIEDMAN, campaign manager for Senator Birch Bayh
JOHN B. GABUSI, campaign director for Congressman Morris K. Udall
PETER D. HART, pollster for Congressman Morris K. Udall
JAMES A. JOHNSON, deputy campaign manager for Senator Walter F. Mondale
HAMILTON JORDAN, campaign manager for Governor Jimmy Carter
MICHAEL KANTOR, adviser to Ambassador R. Sargent Shriver, Jr.; campaign
   manager for Governor Edmund G. Brown, Jr.
ROBERT J. KEEFE, campaign director for Senator Henry M. Jackson
DAVID A. KEENE, Southern coordinator for Governor Ronald Reagan
EDDIE MAHE, JR., executive director of the Republican National Committee
RICHARD MOE, campaign director for Senator Walter F. Mondale
JAMES M. NAUGHTON, political correspondent for the *New York Times*
LYN NOFZIGER, campaign consultant for Governor Ronald Reagan and
   Senator Robert J. Dole
ALAN L. OTTEN, senior national correspondent of the *Wall Street Journal*
JAMES M. PERRY, national affairs columnist for the *National Observer*

JOSEPH L. POWELL, JR., press secretary for Governor Jimmy Carter

JOHN M. QUINN, campaign director for Congressman Morris K. Udall

GERALD RAFSHOON, media director for Governor Jimmy Carter

ELEANOR RANDOLPH, political correspondent for the *Chicago Tribune*

JOHN P. SEARS, campaign director for Governor Ronald Reagan

MARK A. SIEGEL, executive director of the Democratic National Committee

PAUL SIMON, chairman of the committee to draft Senator Hubert H. Humphrey

CHARLES S. SNIDER, campaign director for Governor George C. Wallace

ROBERT M. TEETER, director of research for President Gerald R. Ford

JESSICA TUCHMAN, director of issues and research for Congressman Morris K. Udall

BEN J. WATTENBERG, adviser to Senator Henry M. Jackson

NORMAN E. WATTS, JR., deputy political director for President Gerald R. Ford

RICHARD B. WIRTHLIN, pollster for Governor Ronald Reagan

The Editors

JONATHAN MOORE, director of the Institute of Politics

JANET FRASER, associate director of the Institute of Politics

**Campaign
for President**

Introduction

Jonathan Moore

The 1976 presidential campaign was as confusing as it was exciting. Several factors, particularly when taken in combination, made it dramatically different and complex. There were major changes in party rules for selection of delegates in states, although mainly on the Democratic side—notably the requirements for adequate participation of women and minorities, and for proportional representation in place of the "winner take all" system. There was a proliferation of state primaries up to thirty, seven more than in 1972, and almost a doubling of the number in 1968. For the first time, money was available from the federal treasury to pay for campaign costs—partial and matching in the nomination period, and fully funded in the general election period following the national conventions. There were also new restrictions on financial contributions and expenditures, and a new regulatory agency—the Federal Election Commission—on its shakedown cruise. There was even an incumbent president who had never run for national election before, challenged tenaciously from within his own party. And at one time there were ten serious Democratic candidates in the race, with a former presidential candidate waiting in the wings.

All this made it extremely difficult for candidates for the nomination to plan and fund their campaigns in 1976. Which primaries should they enter? Was there money, energy, and time enough to run in all of them? Some major states complicated matters still further by exploiting a loophole in the proportional representation requirement, bypassing the abolition of the "unit rule" when delegates were elected by congressional district. Contributions couldn't be made by

individuals in amounts over $1,000, which meant that money cost
much more to raise. To qualify for federal matching funds in the primaries, candidates had to raise $5,000 in at least twenty separate
states in amounts of $250 or less. They frequently experienced ex-
cruciating cash flow problems, with chunks of time when they were
broke and forced to skip primaries, lines of credit problems, and
delays in receiving their matching money including a funding suspen-
sion brought about by a Supreme Court decision that challenged and
changed the new rules in the middle of the game. And all the candidates were courting an electorate that seemed more independent in
registration and voting behavior, more unpredictable ideologically,
and more alienated and less willing to vote at all. It was a wild and
woolly year.

It is interesting to look back to the early prognostication about
the Democratic primaries. I can remember discussing over lunch at
Locke-Ober's in Boston before Christmas of 1975 with Johnny
Apple of the *New York Times* and Pat Caddell, who hadn't yet
signed on as Carter's pollster but was thinking about it, whether a
winner would emerge out of the primaries by June or whether there
would have to be a brokered convention in New York in July. Apple
was marginally holding out for a primary winner, I disagreed, Caddell
wouldn't call it, and we wrangled to no conclusion. The political
pundits shortly began to compete hotly but nervously with one
another on both sides of the question. In January, *Newsweek* antici-
pated "high-stakes bargaining" at Madison Square Garden, and
Democratic National Chairman Robert Strauss predicted no final
resolution before the second or third ballot there. The point is, no
one really knew or had any resilient theories. In polls of Democrats
and Independents announced on March 15, Gallup found Humphrey
at 27 percent, Carter 26 percent, Jackson 15 percent, and Wallace
15 percent; and Yankelovich measured Humphrey 32 percent, Carter
28 percent, Wallace 14 percent and Jackson 11 percent. In trial heats
of the same date, Carter was the only leading Democratic candidate
seen beating Ford. In the latter part of March, a Carter-Jackson-Hum-
phrey standoff looked somewhat likely, but no one could predict
with confidence. The circumstances were unprecedented and the factors too volatile.

Carter was the only Democratic candidate who pursued a "run
everywhere" primary approach, part of an overall campaign strategy
he had begun mapping out with remarkable determination four years
earlier. In the early phase, his performance was brilliant. He got a
head start in the Iowa caucus, won a Northern primary for Southern
pride in New Hampshire on February 24, killed off the regional com-

petition and the racial issue in Florida and North Carolina, and beat the Democratic "regulars" in Pennsylvania on April 27. Carter had essentially won the nomination in the first three months by establishing himself as the clear leader of the pack with wide national appeal, while Bayh, Shriver, Harris, Shapp, Wallace, and Jackson were getting eliminated. Bayh was finished after the Massachusetts primary, held on March 2. Wallace, who had placed a close third behind Udall in Massachusetts, was badly hurt in Florida on March 9, where Carter was helped by Udall's absence and with money and votes from anti-Wallace Democrats, and was knocked out in North Carolina on March 23. Jackson's expectations that momentum and money would build up after his win in Massachusetts were frustrated, his third place finish in Florida and his New York victory with only 104 delegates (38 percent, not the landslide he predicted) on April 6 weren't good enough, and he was clobbered in Pennsylvania, on which he had counted heavily.

The latter phase of the Democratic primary period, from early May through early June, began with Humphrey's decision not to run and was characterized by Udall sustaining the only real opposition, by tougher criticism of Carter and more "stop Carter" talk, and by the late entries of Senator Church and Governor Brown. Carter won in D.C., Georgia, and Indiana on May 4, but lost narrowly to Church in Nebraska on May 11, and took a good beating from Brown in Maryland while barely edging Udall in Michigan on May 18. Udall, who had lost a previous crucial squeaker to Carter in Wisconsin on April 6, never won a primary. Carter went on to lose to Church in Idaho, Oregon, and Montana, and to Brown in Nevada and California. But his wins in New Jersey and particularly Ohio on June 8 killed off his opposition, Daley and Meany hurriedly signed on, and it was all over. Carter's losses in the late primaries were too little and too late to hurt him, given his strong Southern support and the fact that even where he lost he was accumulating more delegates due to proportional representation. In addition, the "winners" in this phase, Church and Brown, had started too late to accumulate real delegate strength of their own and couldn't force a brokering situation via delegates denied Carter—sufficient Jackson, Udall, Wallace, and Humphrey support had not materialized, some "favorite sons" didn't run, and not enough uncommitted delegates held firm to block Carter.

Meanwhile, back at the ranch and the Rose Garden, Reagan and Ford were taking turns ravaging and rescuing each other. The president won a narrow victory in New Hampshire, made wider by virtue of the fact that Reagan had failed to avoid being built up as the stronger candidate there, and also won the Massachusetts primary and key victories in Florida and Illinois. Reagan was hurt by his proposal to transfer $90 billion in federal social programs to the states, which looked screwy and was worrisome to social security beneficiaries; by losing the momentum to his incumbent opponent; and by the lack of timely money, which kept him from competing in such primaries as Pennsylvania, West Virginia, Maryland, and Ohio. On the eve of the North Carolina primary, Reagan was virtually broke and virtually finished. But he won North Carolina, went on national television for a half hour with a direct appeal for support, escalated the ideological content of his campaign, and brought in scads of money. He won Texas, Georgia, Alabama, Indiana—helped by Wallace supporters disappointed in the Florida result who crossed over in these "open" primary states—and Nebraska. Ford stabilized by winning his home state of Michigan, where Reagan was again hurt by expectations that were not honored by the voters, and by Democratic crossovers for Ford and Republican votes that had crossed over to Wallace in 1972 but came back to Ford in 1976. Reagan won six out of the next nine states, and, on the final day of the primaries, he cleaned up in California, while Ford won New Jersey and Ohio.

So the race for the G.O.P. nomination was neck and neck—the tally on the first of July gave 1,052 delegates for Ford (78 less than the needed 1,130), 1,018 for Reagan, 91 uncommitted, and 98 to be chosen. It remained uncertain and undecided through June and July, with scrambling for the uncommitted delegates and Reagan's bold—but also perceived as desperate and cynical—choice of Richard Schweiker as his running mate. Then came intensive convention platform jockeying, and the 16C ploy designed to goad Ford to "self-destruct" (in the words of Reagan campaign manager John Sears) by tipping his vice presidential running mate before being named the presidential nominee himself. Ford grimly hung on, held the Mississippi delegation, refused to be drawn into errors the Reagan forces were imaginatively concocting for him, and scraped through. The 1976 nominations for president were decided, and not in the back room, but in the open and across the land.

Both winners were the only ones to run in virtually all of the state primaries. Both were the initial victors in New Hampshire. Both Carter and Ford appealed most to the middle, and best articulated the moderating, reconciling themes in their respective parties. The momentum factor was ragged, but ultimately decisive on both sides. Over twenty-nine million people voted in the thirty state primaries— 20 percent of the voting age population in those states—and 900,000 people participated in caucuses and conventions in twenty-one states

—about 4 percent of the voting age population in those states, according to Kimball Brace in a report prepared for the Democratic National Committee. In both cases, these figures represent significantly higher participation than in prior years.

At the time of the Republican convention in August, Carter led Ford by over thirty percentage points in national polls, with the general election campaign formally to begin on Labor Day. The Democrats had a 48 percent to 23 percent edge in registration over the Republicans, and the inherent advantages of incumbency seemed outweighed by its current liabilities of Watergate, an uncertain economy, and a sense that it was time for a change. But the flexible, complex American political process and its diverse, independent electorate were to confound analysts and prognosticators further in the remaining two months before election day.

When the votes were counted, Carter had 51 percent and Ford 48 percent, and McCarthy almost 1 percent (Lester Maddox, of the American Independent Party, polled a little over 170,000 votes or 0.2 percent). Carter had 297 electoral votes to Ford's 240. Carter "reclaimed" the South, losing only Virginia; the Republican to Democratic shift in the South from 1972 was twenty-six percentage points. Ford won the West, with some exceptions. They split states in the Midwest, Northeast, and New England. But Carter won six of the big ten states—New York, Pennsylvania, Texas, Ohio, Florida, and Massachusetts, with 150 electoral votes, to Ford's four—California, Illinois, Michigan, and New Jersey, with 109 electoral votes.

Carter largely garnered the basic elements of the old Roosevelt coalition. The nonwhites went with him five to one. He won 63 percent of the labor vote. He scored well with the Catholic vote given Ford's hoped-for incursions there. According to Gallup, the economy and economic well-bring were most on the voters' minds and there was no major foreign policy controversy, and this helped Carter. His own persistent emphasis on personal characteristics, values, and style endured, and his theme of reconciliation in race, regional, and religious terms may have held special appeal for an electorate seeking some hope for national cohesion. Robert Rheinhold of the *New York Times* wrote that the campaign boiled down to a contest between incumbency and partisanship, with party numbers and loyalty winning for Carter. Political analyst Michael Barone wrote that the voters narrowly favored an uncertain Democratic future over an unsatisfactory Republican present—"Why not the best?" versus "You could do worse!" William Loeb's Manchester *Union Leader*'s headline the day after the election was: "Shifty Beats Stupid." Clearly, partisan numbers, general public mood, and personality played a greater role in the outcome than did clearly differentiated preferences on issues either on the part of the candidates or the voters.

President Ford did extremely well in reducing Republican defections and in winning the independent vote, but not well enough. From August through October, Gallup divided the voters as follows: Democrats 48 percent, independents 29 percent, Republicans 23 percent. Gallup's postelection tabulation found that independents voted 57 percent for Ford, 38 percent for Carter, and 4 percent for McCarthy. Ford's taking the initiative on the debates helped him, as did Carter's weaker showing during the first debate. But the president's fumble on Eastern Europe while the challenger demonstrated some ease in handling international questions in the second debate hurt him, and Carter claimed subsequently that the exposure he gained by virtue of the debates won him the election.

All the same, one might ask, How was that enormous lead almost blown by the Carter campaign? For one thing, it was inflated at the outset, with Carter and Mondale coming off a peak in New York and laying low for a while, while the president and the Republicans were still getting up off the floor at Kansas City. For another, Carter's efforts to bring together the forces of the Democratic party nationally as distinct from campaigning independently in individual primaries portrayed him both as more liberal and more of a typical politician, more allied with some of those established "Washington" political faces that he had appeared to oppose earlier. The clean, outsider image was tarnished. Also, there were those voters who decided to stick with comfortable, familiar Jerry when they couldn't quite bring themselves to rely on a new Jimmy even though they did find him more interesting. Carter was perhaps more competent, probably more intelligent, but stranger, too—there was more risk there. The *Playboy* interview may have had some effect in this respect, although there's little evidence that it was the reason why people decided to vote for Ford. And Ford's excellent and expensive media campaign helped chip away the Carter lead. Finally, in the general election, Carter was running one-on-one for the first time instead of against the pack. He and his campaign, more tired and ragged, were at the same time under greater pressure. His opponent was the president of the United States; people had the chance to think about that, and an evening-out dynamic went to work.

During the campaign, warnings were rife that half of those eligible to vote wouldn't show up at the polls on November 2. These predictions, like many others, were wrong—54 percent of those eligible voted. But the combination of a new style and face, Watergate, and a cliffhanger campaign were not enough to stop the downward trend in voting—55.4 percent had voted in 1972, 61 percent in 1968, 63 percent in 1960. In 1972, the low turnout was partially explained by the fact that there was a large number of newly enfranchised voters and that the outcome of the election was not in doubt, but neither of those factors was present in 1976. In 1976, 27 percent of Americans over eighteen voted for Carter, 26 percent voted for Ford, and 47 percent stayed home.

There is some disagreement as to how concerned we should be about nonvoting, and it is unclear how much nonvoting is in itself a political act, to what extent the phenomenon is attributable to apathy or alienation, and whether registration requirements constitute a genuine obstacle for nonvoters. A recent study by Peter Hart for the Committee for the Study of the American Electorate holds that registration problems are not the reason why the majority of nonvoters fail to vote; although in Minnesota, which has a system allowing registration up to election day, over 70 percent of those eligible voted in 1976. Also, there are varying patterns: although there is a continuing decline of voting in the North, there is increased voting in the South. In Texas, 500,000 more votes were cast in 1976 than in 1972. Carter won by only 150,000 votes in Texas, while Ford partisans there, as elsewhere in the country, disconcertingly rooted for a low turnout. Currently, a lot of study and analysis is being given to this problem, and so far the results are inconclusive.

We now have an electoral process that some professional politicians and analysts believe requires serious campaigns to begin two years or more before election day. This means spending almost a full year in nonstop campaigning; candidates end up exhausted, if not burned out; and almost half of the electorate are no-shows. This system can't be all good, but there is considerable question as to how to improve it, and skepticism about where reform heaped on reform will lead us.

The current system is so complex and demanding that it may be discouraging potential qualified candidates for the presidency far in advance. Added to the deterrent posed by the prodigious difficulty and personal risk of the job are the intensified demands of seeking it. We may be in danger of losing more competent, balanced leaders in preference to a compulsively ambitious and hyperactive breed—electing campaigners rather than governors, speculators rather than managers. People may be not voting because they are turned off by the seemingly chaotic and confusing nature of the process or are just plain unimpressed by the choices available. The electorate does get a chance to see the toughness, judgment, and stamina of the candidates tested by the rigors of extended campaigning throughout the nation. But attributes required in the presidency include the serious reflection, strategic planning, and managerial acumen needed to grasp and anticipate the manifold problems of our society and to conduct policies to resolve them. These qualities are not tested by the frenetic, reactive, manipulative character of campaigns, which place little premium and considerable risk on the serious treatment of substantive issues ideally essential to a governance shared by the elected and the electorate. The new campaign laws diminish the corrupting influence of money in politics by a combination of public subsidies, restrictions on private contributions, and disclosure of who's giving how much to whom. They assure easier entry tied to demonstrated support and equalized spending for less well-known candidates; the federal matching funds enabled Carter to mount his assault in the primaries. But the new finance limitations may also be unduly aiding incumbents, crowding constitutional rights, and constraining the educational value of campaigns and grassroots participation. Television is at the same time crucially important, terribly expensive, and sadly unenlightening. The political parties, not yet obsolete, are encouraged in their obsolescence by the very nature of contemporary political campaigns.

But there is no perfection to be wrought, no grand design or ultimate rationalization, and credible prescriptions are elusive. The American people can't be coddled into greater or more serious political participation, and the viability of the overall process will depend more on our cultural and spiritual dimensions, more on the quality of leadership of both the leaders and the led in the peculiarly reciprocating dynamic of American democracy, than on rules and regulations negotiated by experts and lawmakers. What is needed includes careful research and analysis by independent authorities of the experience we've had and the evidence collected; consideration of improvements by public interest groups with a detachment that belies an overly protective attitude toward reform already pressed; and further legislation by a Congress unhindered by its unhappily precedented interest in saving its individual skins. Such further effort can achieve a modestly more rational and workable process, still pluralistic and flexible, if it is cautious rather than impetuous in its approach, and if it deals with all the pieces together that make up the whole.

The arguments against a national primary seem strong enough to reject it in favor of the continuing mix of caucus and primary states, but the 1976 experience supports a reduced number of the latter, perhaps with the testing of a regional primary concept in one part of the country or another but not imposed as a national system.

There are good reasons for affirmative action and proportional representation in delegate selection. Crossover primaries argue for elimination. Federal matching money in the primaries will work better if administrative red tape can be restricted and if the Federal Election Commission can be restrained from becoming the Gargantua of regulatory agencies. Making more funds available and raising expenditure ceilings in certain categories could help strengthen the role of the political parties and of grassroots participation and help weaken the incumbency advantage. The proliferation of political action committees and independent expenditures needs further examination. Ingenuity is needed to devise adequate and cheaper television access. If a direct popular election replaces the electoral college, in order to avoid the disadvantages and cost of a run-off in the event no candidate receives 40 percent of the vote cast, the House and Senate should decide the election in joint session with each member casting one vote. If the electoral college is retained, the electors probably should be eliminated. Finally, careful attention needs to be given to the incentives and disincentives surrounding low voting, partly by more party and grassroots activity mentioned above, and partly by easing registration requirements.

*   *   *

Two selected topics that have bearing on the future character of our political process, and about which there is new information and revealing comment in this volume, deserve some further attention. The first is the relevance and role of issues, ideology, and personality in the recent presidential campaigning. The second is the effect of the nomination struggles in the two parties on their respective capacities to prevail in the general election of 1976.

Substantive issues were of marginal significance in the '76 campaign—even though their importance compared to candidate and party traits had risen during 1960–1972. Consistently, their treatment tended to be superficial and manipulative. This was the first campaign since 1936 when a major foreign policy or national security issue did not dominate. Detente, Henry Kissinger, and Panama fired up for a while in the Republican contest, but not in the general election. Gallup reported that inflation and unemployment, cited by Americans as "the most important issue facing the country," rose between April 1976 and the week before the November election by nine and seven percentage points, 62 percent and 78 percent, respectively. This preoccupation undoubtedly had some influence on the outcome, particularly in light of poll findings that voters perceived Carter and the Democratic party as better able to handle the economy and other domestic concerns. But it was hardly decisive, and failed to generate radical differences in the policy positions of the two candidates or especially promising policy proposals for dealing with economic problems.

The relative insignificance of substantive policy issues can be attributed to several factors. The voters don't place a high premium on them, perhaps because they don't entirely trust what they hear candidates say about them and have greater confidence in their ability to get some feeling for how generally capable and reliable a given candidate is. There are some hard core issues pursued by hard core groups, but they tend to cancel out. Voters tend naturally to be confused by intricate and intransigent governmental problems, and once they get a general idea of where a candidate stands—how moderate, how extreme—that's likely to be enough. Indeed, the inherent complexity of most public policy issues inhibits their role in political campaigns. Candidates are very wary of getting in over their heads or getting hit over the head on complicated, controversial substance. Jimmy Carter chose "fuzziness" over "specificity," and apparently was right. Ronald Reagan took an ambitious shot at substantive policy innovation, trying to save ninety billion federal dollars on social programs by pushing them off on the states, and he was wrong. Governor Jerry Brown admitted, "A little vagueness goes a long way in this business." Finally, the media, particularly television, is not equipped to handle serious issues competently. One of the great ironies of the campaign was media response on several occasions when they had been successful in goading a candidate into detailed policy positions—they were the first to zap him, or they didn't accurately or adequately cover him.

Ideology also appears to have played a secondary role in the 1976 campaigns. The middle—or everywhere—was the place to be. A CBS–New York Times poll in early September 1976 found that the electorate, when asked, divided itself along conventional ideological lines into 25 percent liberal, 41 percent moderate, 34 percent conservative. Americans, however, were not inclined to apply doctrinal measures to candidacies. The candidates returned the favor by avoiding undue typing of themselves. There were exceptions, of course, but Wallace described himself as a "populist," and Udall stopped describing himself as a "liberal." Ronald Reagan's campaign took on more of an ideological bent when he went on national television and badly needed money, but earlier he was criticizing Ford for not being nicer to the Communist Chinese. I can remember a telephone call from pollster and political analyst Walter DeVries, shortly before the North Carolina primary, to report that the self-identified Carter supporters he had just interviewed there split into thirds when asked whether they planned to vote for him because he was liberal, moderate, or conservative; Carter's candidacy never lost this characteristic. A CBS—*New York Times* election day poll reported the voters' perceptions of Carter along ideological lines as liberal 32 percent, moderate 30 percent, conservative 19 percent. The problems the nation faces are sufficiently complex as not to bend easily to ideological characterizations or prescriptions, and individual voters take different positions on different sets of issues that, taken together, are not congenial according to traditional ideological measures.

In any event, we don't have candidates who are appealing to the electorate on the basis of a cohesively developed and thoroughly articulated political philosophy. This is understandable, given the complexity of the above-mentioned problems our society faces, as well as its pluralistic and pragmatic character, but the future consequences of this deficiency are unknown. In American politics, we have little real sense of continuing commitment to a body of thought or principle. The name of the game is, if we can win, that's it. We don't know yet what this attitude may mean to the vitality and effectiveness of our democratic system, or whether it signals a broken circuit between our political process and our governmental process.

Granted, there are vaguer and softer "issues" that voters feel strongly about that play a major role in our election process. Attitudes concerning dissatisfaction with big government, distrust of Washington, perceptions of moral decline, assessments based on "traditional American values," and preferences about who is better equipped to handle which national problems are examples of opinions that overlap issues, ideology, and personality, perhaps combining aspects of each. Personal attributes obviously are tested by issue preferences and ideological standards, and positions on issues tend to project individual qualities. But personality dominates. When you get to personal style, character, ability, you're where the action is—for the candidates, the media, the voters, the campaign industry.

The greatest interest seems to be in efforts to project and market (on the delivery side) and to observe and intuit (on the consumer side) who the candidate is, what he's worth, and what skills he has. How decent, intelligent, tough, is he? Is he an egomaniac, seduced by power, or secure in his own identity? What kind of judgment does he have, what managerial talent? What capacity for recognizing and attracting able people, sorting out priorities, applying grace under pressure? And so forth. Carter beat out Ford on perceptions of competence, intelligence, and concern for the average citizen. He was preferred on strong ability, seen as being more colorful, interesting, and imaginative, and as having leadership qualities. He deliberately tried to contrast himself to Ford's dullness, questionable competence, and complacency with the way things were. Ford was regarded as stronger on experience, more moderate, more predictable, and "nonwaffling." Carter was regarded by some as weird and Ford by some as boring. These kinds of perceptions, opinions, and hunches are what a great deal of the time, energy, money, words, and pictures were all about in 1976. We can expect more of the same.

The debates illustrate the general point. A lot of people watched—according to Gallup, between 67 percent and 70 percent viewed the three debates. Whether the debates determined the result (virtually anything can, in a close campaign), they were not enlightening on the substance of our problems, and not illuminating on the issue positions of the candidates. Neither were they, except erratically, distinguished along ideological lines. They were opportunistic and tactical, characterized by statistical fencing and recitation of memorized facts and cliches. Only now and then was the rigidity and posturing broken in favor of a flash of spontaneous behavior or special insight. And the media, unsatisfied with this, demeaned the experience further by concentrating on who "won" and who "lost," shaping public opinion by simplistic verdicts even further removed from the potential value of the debates.

They had political impact, to be sure. After the first debate, both sides agreed that the two most significant points scored were, by Ford—as governor of Georgia, Carter sent government costs and indebtedness up; and, by Carter—if he had to account for the actions of the Democrat Congress, then Ford was responsible for the Nixon administration. Ford's overly celebrated Eastern Europe "misstatement" hurt him, and triggered even more interesting sideshows: the president's waste of precious time in delayed explanation of his error and stabilization of its damage; and Carter's over-reacting attack on Ford's blunder, which also took too much time to stop. This is not to suggest that we shouldn't have debates, which along with other evidence provide guidance to the voters, who on this occasion saw Ford as they thought they knew him, and, getting better introduced to Carter, found him more reassuring and less scary than he might ha' been. Rather, it is to say that they really don't work well enough and that they have greater utility for "candidate perception" than in substantive or philosophical terms.

This brings us to the second topic selected for further attention here: how well the Democrats and Republicans each handled the threats to their prospects in November that are inherent in the heated competition for the nomination. One of the most compelling and suspenseful questions of our quadrennial competitions for the Oval Office is how far the party gladiators will go in destroying each other. After the internecine phase is completed, it remains to be discovered if the wounds are bindable and the divisions bridgeable by party loyalty discovered in the nick of time. Major contenders may give energetic support to the victor, provide minimal backing while plotting another try four years hence, or dare all in a third party split. This is not a new phenomenon, but it is particularly relevant given the frailty of political parties in general and the perilous health of the G.O.P. in particular, and it can be argued that in 1976 Carter won and Ford lost the general election in the primaries.

The Democrats had to live with the prospect of Gene McCarthy all the way through, watching him, part noble, part querulous, alone and palely loitering. The worry was that he would get the 5 percent of the national vote he claimed would be a sign of voter disaffection with the two major political parties and cost Carter the election in proving something that had already been quite powerfully demonstrated. He never flinched at playing the spoiler and got on the ballot in twenty-nine states. Near the end of September, Gallup put McCarthy at 4 percent of the popular vote, and most analysts figured he was drawing considerably more from Carter than from Ford. In the end, he received 680,000 votes, or slightly less than 1 percent, and probably cost the Democratic nominee four states—Maine, Oklahoma, Iowa, and Oregon, for twenty-six electoral votes. McCarthy didn't poll well enough for Carter to lose Massachusetts, Pennsylvania, Texas, and Ohio, and his margin was not great enough to credit him for the Ford wins in New Jersey, Illinois, and Michigan.

Given McCarthy's activities, the Democrats might have been just as happy if George Wallace had also split off on his own, flying the American Independence party banner. But one of the former Georgia governor's most prodigious accomplishments during 1976 was the way he knocked off the governor of Alabama, just the way he said he would. The expectations for Wallace were inflated this time around, put by some as high as 700 convention delegates early in the betting, and even at 400 by the beginning of April, but he ended the primaries with 168. He repeatedly ruled out a third party race, which hurt him and helped Carter, and his challenge was simply not as threatening as in the past. He did well in the Massachusetts primary, just missing second place. But sometime Udall campaign aide Ira Jackson and I went to the Wallace rally on the eve of the Bay State vote at Loew's Orpheum Theatre in Boston, where there was a lot of noise and a big crowd, the troop of local busing advocates, and the display of tough confidence. The next day there were impressed reviews in the media. But the old zing, the electric emotion, wasn't there, the candidate was hurt and tired, the message had been sent too often, and you could see in his eyes he didn't believe it enough himself anymore. The Florida primary was the coup de gras, but Wallace waited until June 9 to declare for Carter, which wasn't too late to be of help, keeping the South solid.

In early March, Hubert Humphrey led Wallace, Carter, and Jackson in that order in polls of Democrats. In late March, he was still waiting for the back room in New York in July, the brokers' sentimental favorite, and there was some thought that if Scoop Jackson did well in April in New York and Pennsylvania, Humphrey might be used to stop him. But Humphrey had some nagging, if mild, Watergate-reminiscent problems, his health was a problem, this was not the year to stay out of the primaries, and the other candidates didn't fragment the front runner enough. After Pennsylvania, he finally decided not to enter any of the final primaries still open to him. The "anybody but Carter" movement had fizzled—if it had succeeded, it would have threatened the Democrats seriously in November, because of Southern resentment. So the Democrats reunited. Udall and Jackson were adequately on board for the postconvention campaign, and Jerry Brown's lackluster support was just enough not to hurt. The base was largely protected, the ranks were mostly closed.

The Republicans didn't fare as well, within as well as without. Governor Reagan shut off suggestions early on that he bolt the party and run on a conservative ticket, perhaps picking up Wallace and Connally forces, and stuck with the G.O.P. all the way through. But despite the concern of such senior Republican counselors as Bryce Harlow that such a fight might "disembowel" the party, he challenged an incumbent Republican president hard and almost justified the heresy by pulling it off. It is clear that in certain respects the Reagan race helped Ford's campaign and the Republican cause in the fall. It forced the president, who had not previously mounted a national campaign, to get his act together, and it gave the Republicans more media exposure. As a result, Ford had a significant victory under his belt on Labor Day. But the harm was probably greater. A sitting president was criticized on all fronts—national security, the economy, Watergate—and nearly humiliated by his own party. After seemingly having won the nomination, he then watched helplessly as it slipped almost all the way away and finally captured it because his challenger fell shy and couldn't fake him into enough mistakes to blow it.

Reagan averted a revolt by his partisans against Ford at the convention, but he forced Ford to put control of the convention above everything else. The president was pinned down by and pleading with the right wing of a party of badly diminished numbers, when he should have been broadening his base of appeal. And although Reagan campaigned for Ford in the fall, his performance depended too heavily on complaints that the Ford camp wasn't handling him right, on low-key endorsement of the president personally and on high-key support for conservative candidates for the Senate and the House. The Republicans only had the White House left to lose—they were already terribly weak in the Congress and the state capitols. But again they appeared to be more the victims of their internal differences than were their adversaries when the chips were down, at least marginally, but in a situation where the margin meant everything.

The vice presidential sweepstakes expose the point. Once Carter had his nomination in the bag, he had plenty of time to work deliberately on his choice of vice president, which he did in such a way as to pull the traditional resources of his party together and pick a running mate who was a good complement on the ticket and perceived to be capable of serving as president himself. The Republicans didn't have the same assets of time and unity. In late July, Governor Reagan showed his capacity for the bold move and his appreciation of the need for competency and base-broadening in a running mate by his selection of Richard Schweiker. Ironically, he was incapable in August of helping Ford serve the same goals, by signaling only the name of Bob Dole as a choice acceptable to him in an environment of need and vulnerability for the just-nominated president. The arguments about this will go on interminably, of course. The press jumped all over Ford when Dole was announced. Dole firmed up the farm states and reduced Republican defections. But how about those additional independent voters Ford needed and didn't get? The senator did not fare well in his debate with Mondale, and Gallup personality ratings persistently put Mondale well in front of his counterpart. The Carter camp, based on polling results, ran negative advertisements on Dole, and Elmo Roper claimed his voter motivation studies showed that Carter could have increased his victory margin over Ford by exploiting Mondale more as a political asset. It is correct that few voters will decide a vote on positive or negative feelings about the second person on the ticket. It is less convincing to argue that in reaching a choice for president, some voters are not likely to factor in the judgment and stature exhibited by a candidate in the selection of his running mate.

*   *   *

The Institute of Politics first sponsored a conference of campaign decisionmakers and published a book out of the discussions, *Campaign '72*, edited by Ernest May and Janet Fraser, four years ago. This project was so successful that it was automatically decided to undertake it anew. Ms. Fraser, the institute's associate director, again coordinated the conference and again has done almost all the editing for this volume.

Invitations were extended to approximately thirty-five campaign practitioners, and twenty-eight were able to attend. Every major 1976 campaign was represented, as well as the Democratic and Republican National Committees. Five political journalists agreed to serve as moderators, and the ground to be covered was divided into five sessions, running from Friday afternoon through Sunday morning, December 3–5, 1976, and covering the Republican primaries and convention, the Democratic primaries and convention, and the general election. The participants sat around a square of tables in the library of the Harvard Faculty Club. About a hundred faculty, students, journalists, assorted campaign aficionados, officials from state and local government, and other friends of the institute were invited to attend the conference as observers with the understanding that the proceedings were off the record until the transcript had been published. The sessions were taped, and all the participants—the authors —were subsequently asked to review the edited transcript and make changes in their comments for accuracy and clarification, but not to change the meaning or to rewrite for style.

What makes this book unique is that it was written, so to speak, by those who actually shared responsibility for what happened—the campaign decisionmakers themselves—and that they reconstruct the events of presidential election year 1976 together, jointly, so that the story is developed as an integrated whole, rather than by separate versions of competing campaigns simply juxtaposed. The back and forth discussion and the intervention of differing perspectives largely accomplish what was intended in exploring how the process worked, in considering the tradeoffs and competing priorities, and in analyzing the strategic and tactical decisions at various stages, their motivation and their consequences. Extensive candor is demonstrated, and a spirit of sharing experiences and seeking the truth achieved.

But there are some shortcomings experienced in this format that the reader should be aware of before reading the book. First, although there were few absences, at some points not all of the participants were present; some had to arrive late or leave early. To wit, John Sears was only present during discussions of the Republican primaries; Eleanor Randolph didn't arrive until the first session on the

Democratic primaries; Hamilton Jordan didn't arrive until midway through the discussion of the Democratic primaries; and neither Mr. Jordan nor Jody Powell was able to be present at the wrap up discussion on the general election.

Second, because the participants were principal actors in the campaigns, they may tend to rationalize their decisions or the performance of their candidate, or fall prey to seductive recollection. Some may also on occasion view events differently because of the outcome and their personal relationship to it. It is very difficult, for instance, for people from some of the competing campaigns to speak up boldly when asked about the "stop Carter" movement with other people, who had won and were then assuming power, sitting across the table—life goes on, there are important battles ahead, and work to do in the new administration.

Third, readers should be alert for specific instances in the transcript where the discussion is too superficial, moves so fast as to omit an important aspect, appears unduly self-serving, or lacks adequate explanation. For instance, on pages 36–40 there is mention of the Reagan $90 billion proposal, but not adequate detail of what the proposal was or its specific impact on the campaign. On page 67, there is no identification of what the five or six issues are that are being discussed in terms of misperceptions and gaps between Carter and Reagan. We are reminded on page 82 that the transcript lacks discussion about Carter's extraordinary ability to sell people early on his ability to win, without any available evidence to prove it. It is not clear on page 107 whether Governor Brown really believed he had a chance in a brokered convention or if he was trying to position himself for 1980. And on pages 119–120, it is perplexing that the voters perceived Ford as substantially more liberal than Carter according to "traditional American values" when Carter argued for sizeable cuts in the defense budget, supported the decriminalization of marijuana, and took a softer position on abortion than did Ford.

In conclusion, gratitude is expressed to the institute staff, which worked faithfully and hard on both the conference and this publication, to members of the institute's Student Advisory Committee who escorted participants while they were in Cambridge and assisted with the recording of the sessions, and to Christopher Arterton, Ira Jackson, David Keene, and Tom Ottenad for their advice on this introduction. Most of all, the editors wish to thank the moderators and practitioners for sharing their experience, analysis, commitment, and humor with each other, the Institute of Politics, and the readers of this book.

Chapter 1

The Republican Nomination

Ford's Decision to Run. Reagan Challenge. White House Response to Reagan Challenge. Timing of Reagan Decision. Rockefeller Withdrawal. Reagan Primary Strategy. Ford Primary Strategy. Reagan Contingency Strategy. Paying the Bills. Closing Primaries. Campaign Issues. Selection of Schweiker. White House Perspective. Republican Convention. Question 16C. "Morality in Government" Plank. Ford Convention Strategy. Selection of Dole. Decisive Factors.

JAMES M. NAUGHTON (political correspondent, *New York Times*): What we'd like to examine first is how the 1976 presidential campaign on the Republican side took shape before the nomination was decided. For the sake of convenience, we'll divide the early campaign into three parts: first, the preprimary and precaucus period, when basic strategy was presumably being designed by both Mr. Ford and Mr. Reagan; second, the early primaries, which the president won through North Carolina and then lost when the campaign became a real contest; and finally, the period from North Carolina leading up to the convention, when it was a definite scramble for the nomination. Given the state of the Republican party in early 1975 and the likelihood that the nomination might not amount to all that much, why did each side really want it? [to Michael Duval] Why, for example, did President Ford, after suggesting in his 1973 vice presidential confirmation hearings that he was not interested in running for president, decide that he was in 1975?

FORD'S DECISION TO RUN

MICHAEL DUVAL (special counsel to Ford): I don't know what made the president decide to run. I think it was a highly personal decision. At the time of his vice presidential hearings in 1973, of course, he was clearly not thinking about becoming president. There would have been a certain element of arrogance in his assuming such a thing then; in 1975, when he decided to run, the context of the times was very different. Also, I think he was motivated to run by his desire to accomplish the three important goals he had set for himself on assuming the presidency in 1974: first, to restore trust in the White House and in government; second, to conclude the Viet Nam war in a manner that did not do severe damage to our national security or foreign policy; and three, to cope with the growing recession. I think he was motivated to run by his sense of what he could contribute in the next four years.

NAUGHTON: What were the strategic judgments that were being made in 1975 about the prospects of the president?

ROBERT M. TEETER (director of research for Ford): It was unknown in 1975 whether or not Governor Reagan was going to run, and there was almost nothing known about who the Democratic candidate might be. I suspect that the president may have had some questions when he took office in 1974 about the nature of the problems facing him and how he would handle them, but I think that by 1975 he felt strongly that he understood the problems that were facing the country and that he was better prepared to deal with them than anybody else. I became directly involved in the campaign discussions in 1975 at a time when it was a strong possibility that Governor Reagan would run, but not a sure thing. In the late summer and fall of 1975, I suspect that the White House was doing things with an eye to the possibility of a Reagan campaign, and thinking about how to discourage it, and how to handle it if it should become a fact. There may have been more attention given to where the president went and what he did than there otherwise would have been.

REAGAN CHALLENGE

NAUGHTON: John Sears, you were offered the opportunity to work in the president's campaign and chose instead to work in Governor Reagan's. Why did you do that? And why did Governor Reagan, who has always spoken of the need for party unity, challenge an incumbent president of his own party?

JOHN P. SEARS (campaign manager for Reagan): I still don't think to this day that Governor Reagan has done anything but help the party's unity. Indeed, I think the race itself was an immeasurable help to the Republican party. Two years ago, the party was in no shape to run a national campaign, and I think that it did as well as it did in 1976 because it had a race. I can't speak for Governor Reagan, but I know that I felt that the Republican party, if it was going to be an important party in this country after what happened at Watergate, had a responsibility to demonstrate that it still had the wherewithal as a political institution to search its ranks and have an open discussion about who ought to be nominated for president. It could thereby convince the American people that though it might be small in numbers, it still had the facility to go about its business in an appropriate and right fashion, in terms of nominating somebody who could serve as president of the United States. Mr. Ford's presence in the Oval Office created great political problems for us in our effort to secure the nomination for Governor Reagan—from the first day to the last. Mr. Ford, in most respects, was a unique incumbent. In the past when people had died in office and vice presidents had become presidents, the vice presidents had at least had national exposure in campaigns and had developed some image while in office. Mr. Ford, because of the circumstances of his becoming president, did not have that kind of exposure or image. There was feeling in the party that the party itself had not been able to pass on him as a presidential candidate. Regardless of the outcome of the nomination process for 1976, we felt that our participation in it could be well justified in terms of the good of the party and would not be divisive. We resolved to do all that we could to make sure that the party would not be harmed as a result of the race. I still think that these considerations were proper ones at the time. We certainly were disappointed that we didn't get the nomination, but we didn't regret our contribution to the process. At a very early stage, we all had the feeling that if we could lick the problem of being nominated, we could get elected; but we had, as I said, great difficulty about the nomination. Mr. Ford was not disliked by most of the people who were supporting Mr. Reagan, even those who were close to him. Most of us had been in politics previously, and many of those supporting Mr. Ford were still friends of ours. We thought that in that kind of atmosphere we could keep this thing from getting out of hand. During the race, there was much anticipation of some serious division in the party—indeed, even today there is a great deal of talk of that. It didn't happen all the way through the race, and I don't think it will happen now. Things turned out as we hoped they would, except for our not getting nominated.

LYN NOFZIGER (campaign consultant for Reagan and Dole): One reason we got into it was that we felt it was winnable, even though we knew we were behind. We looked at surveys and so forth, and it appeared that if we did our job, it was possible. I don't think we would have gone in if we had felt there was no way to win it. But beyond that, Governor Reagan was concerned about the direction in which the Ford administration was moving, and we felt that all the pressures on him were from the liberal side. There were huge deficits, and there was a foreign policy that the governor did not agree with. Most of us felt that if the governor were a candidate, we could rally the conservatives and, win or lose, could move the party back in the direction we thought it ought to be going in. In retrospect, I think we were correct. I think that there was a possibility that we might have won it, and I think that in the process we did move President Ford to the right. In addition, something we hadn't counted on, we made the president a much better candidate than he would have otherwise been.

RICHARD B. WIRTHLIN (pollster for Reagan): The governor didn't make a hard decision to run until the end of September 1975. However, as early as July 1974, we had taken some national soundings, using Senator Edward Kennedy [of Massachusetts] as a stalking horse. At that time, when Ford was still vice president, the difference between a Reagan-Kennedy and a Ford-Kennedy race was only 1 percent. When Richard Nixon left office [in August 1974], the governor's position was simple: it was best for all of us if President Ford could succeed in uniting the country. At that point the governor's presidential program was put on ice. Then, about March 1975, we did a national survey that indicated that the president was not putting it together and that there was a difference of only thirteen points separating President Ford and Governor Reagan among Republicans in a hypothetical primary race. In addition, the data indicated that none of the then front-running Democrats—Humphrey, Muskie, McGovern—maintained a terribly strong position. We assessed the governor's political strength on the basis of his acceptability among various groups, and we did the same for Ford, as well as for some possible Democratic opponents. At that time, the president held the edge, but one not sufficiently large to discourage active interest in a possible Reagan campaign. In September 1975, on the basis of a large survey, 2,000-plus in interviews, I was asked to determine four things: one, what were the possibilities of Reagan's winning the nomination; two, would such a challenge split the Republican party if Reagan won the nomination, and if so, would Republicans come back to the winner in the general election; three, what were the issues of concern, and could they be used more effectively by Reagan than Ford in building a winning coalition; and four, what might be the nature of that coalition.

Concerning the prospects of winning the Republican primary, we found that Gerald Ford mustered only a slim majority among the party faithful. Republicans viewed Ronald Reagan as more "competent" and "stronger," equally as "safe" but not as "kind" as the incumbent president. The governor, nevertheless, was extremely anxious that the Republican party not be disrupted, and in fact the evidence then indicated that a Reagan challenge would not split the party. For instance, we found that about 73 percent of those who voted for Ford over Reagan in a hypothetical primary would come back and vote for Reagan when we paired him against any of the series of Democratic opponents, and the same thing among Reagan supporters. Further, 60 percent of the Republicans felt that a Reagan candidacy would be healthy for the party.

The study also indicated that the issues were very conducive to a Reagan candidacy. Two factors that had seared the conscience of the American electorate were Viet Nam and Watergate. One of the attitudinal consequences of the importance of these two issues was, of course, an increase in alienation and cynicism, and a great reluctance to accept the Washington bureaucracy. In 1964, when Goldwater ran for president, 76 percent of the electorate said that they could trust government to do what was right, always or most of the time. When we did the survey in September 1975, only 36 percent believed that they could trust government to do what was right, almost always or most of the time. There was a solid majority which rejected the bureaucratic liberalism and policies of the past decade. Therefore, we felt that the incumbency did not have the political leverage that had given it such power earlier. In regard to the general election, when paired against a series of Democratic contenders, Governor Reagan ran almost as well as Ford, garnering support which ranged between 43 and 49 percent, with the Democratic vote strength at that juncture appearing fluid and vulnerable. The most probable winning coalition for Reagan in a general election consisted of the Republican core, good Southern support, and "soft" Democrats in the middle age, middle income, nonprofessional occupations who were rubbed raw with taxes and what they perceived to be wasteful welfare payments.

NAUGHTON: What was the attitude of the Republican National Committee at this time? What did they think of the likelihood of the challenge? Were they trying to prevent one, encourage one, or what?

EDDIE MAHE, JR. (executive director, Republican National Committee): We had no position on the challenge. We took the attitude early on that we would continue to be supportive of the Republican administration that was in the White House, namely that of President Ford, but that in terms of the committee itself and the allocation of time and resources, we would be organizationally neutral throughout the campaign. There was great division within the committee and the staff about the ultimate impact of Governor Reagan's challenge. Some shared the view that it would be nothing but beneficial; others, particularly during the months of June and July preceding the convention, were quite convinced that the challenge would make it impossible to get the party back together. But we neither encouraged nor discouraged Governor Reagan.

NAUGHTON: Was it your sense at that time that there was a chance of winning the election? Did it depend on who the candidate was?

MAHE: I don't think any of us [in the RNC] ever doubted our capacity to win the presidential election. We did not feel that very many of the Democrats who were talking about making this race had the capacity for putting together the necessary coalitions.

SEARS: When Governor Reagan agreed to run for the nomination, I think that one other factor was definitely in his mind. During late 1974 and early 1975, there had been a great deal of discussion in some quarters about starting a third party, and he felt that his running would encourage that sentiment to die away, and [would] keep the Republican party together. Realizing that the Republican party was small to begin with, he could certainly not afford to split its numbers once again. If he did not run in the Republican party for the nomination, other people might be encouraged to go off and start their own party; whereas if he ran, he could hold most people in the Republican party.

NOFZIGER: When we [Reagan people] put this thing together in July 1975, there was no final assurance even that Gerald Ford would seek election. There was still talk that he might not, and had he not, of course, it would have been an entirely different thing. I think that was a consideration in the governor's decision.

WHITE HOUSE RESPONSE TO REAGAN CHALLENGE

NAUGHTON: How did the White House respond to the likelihood of a challenge from Governor Reagan? There always seemed to be conflicting signs—on the one hand, they seemed to ignore it, and on the other hand, they seemed to be frightened to death of it.

DUVAL: I was alone in this view, but I felt very strongly that the challenge by Governor Reagan was most important and beneficial in giving President Ford a campaign capability that had a chance of winning in November. I do not think that the president's campaign effort would have been nearly so effective in the general election without the challenge from Governor Reagan; and if the challenge had dissipated or disappeared after North Carolina, we [Ford people] would have been, in my judgment, much less effective in the general election. Although there were very dark days in May, June, July, and early August [1976], and there was a real fear that we could lose the nomination, I continued to feel that there was no sense in getting the nomination if we couldn't win. The benefit of the decisions that Governor Reagan's challenge forced the Ford campaign to make far outweighed the lack of sleep and the weight loss of the challenge itself. I felt that postnomination unity would be a function of the perceived ability of the candidate to win, and all the rest of the bad feelings and rivalries would just fall by the side. If the candidate was perceived as being able to win, the party would pull behind him. And I think that's what did happen.

NAUGHTON: You said that yours was not the prevalent view in the White House. What was?

DUVAL: I think people had conflicting feelings. There were a lot of people associated both in the White House and in the primary effort who had a very difficult time coping with the challenge and argued that we would have been better off working on the general election and not having to worry about this. But, in my view, the challenge forced us to make the hard decisions about people, organization, and discipline that would be needed in the general election.

NAUGHTON: But there seemed to be a deliberate effort to steer Reagan off, to entice former Reagan allies into the Ford camp, to make overtures to people like John Sears, to make a number of trips to California, to have fundraisers and others events seemingly designed to show how popular and powerful the president was. Didn't all this suggest that, somehow or other, the president might persuade Reagan not to run?

DUVAL: My feeling is very personal and perhaps uninformed, but I feel that the kinds of decisions you need to make in the primary period are very different from what's needed in the general election period. There is a compelling argument to be made, in my judgment, for a different leadership in the primary fight and the general election fight. The people that were involved in winning the nomination obviously wanted to do everything to win that bout, but I think that the decisions that were made to do that often worked against our best interest in the general election.

TIMING OF REAGAN DECISION

DAVID S. BRODER (associate editor, *Washington Post*): Did the Ford efforts that Jim Naughton just described have any effect at all on Reagan's decisionmaking? Related to that, what was the critical factor in the timing of Reagan's decision to run? There appeared to be great pressure on Reagan to get into the race quickly if he were going to get in. Was the matter of his timing in any way critical in what happened later on?

NOFZIGER: The thing that I always found interesting was that the Ford people, even those who were supposed to have been close to Reagan, completely misjudged their man. Reagan is not a man that you pressure. He's a man that you win with kindness, and the efforts in California to take his organization away from him did nothing but anger him and heighten his resolve. Also, the Ford people's efforts to get California were not very good—I think that they had more effect on reporters than anything else.

SEARS: When you're undertaking a race against an incumbent in your own party, and also having to come out of that race in shape to run in a national campaign, there are a number of things that you weigh very carefully. Timing becomes a very important matter, much more than in other races, where the conditions are different. A race against an incumbent is like the classic heavyweight boxing match between a very large fellow with a good left hand—and if he ever hits you with it, you're dead—and the challenger who's a little lighter, but perhaps a little smoother on his feet, who can dance a little bit. The challenger's job is to keep the play of the game going and maybe tire the other fellow and jab a lot. We [Reagan people] were, of course, in the latter position.

Early on, the governor was under a great deal of pressure to get into the race, or else there would be no race. We couldn't really see the value of that reasoning. It seemed to us that we should try to make the race into our game—in other words, that we should take steps that would better our chances. There was a certain fear of the governor's candidacy in the White House. Also, in any long, drawn-out situation, we were always vulnerable to the power of the office being used against us. So, in our view, we were not making an incorrect judgment to bide our time about announcing whether he might run. We did not feel, contrary to what people were telling us, that we were going to lose support by that. Through the summer of 1975, as far as we could see, Ford supporters were out asking people for support, and in many parts of the country people were withholding it. Those that weren't were, in our view, mainly people that probably would have gone to Ford utlimately anyway. The timing of our announcement was very much geared to trying to get into the race at an appropriate time before the primary season started, wherein we could make a fast run in the primaries and not have to be in the race so long that the powers that the president has to change the character of the issues could be used against us. All these factors dictated an announcement sometime in the middle to late fall, and we did announce on November 20. This gave us enough time before the New Hampshire primary [in February 1976] to come at that in strong shape, living off some of the publicity from the announcement. All in all, if there was any mistake made about that, perhaps we should have waited a week or so longer. But we were under severe pressure for most of the year to announce well before that. Reagan was under direct pressure to make his intentions known as early as spring.

DAVID A. KEENE (Southern coordinator for Reagan): The governor was getting a great deal of pressure from people who were either prospective supporters or active supporters of a potential Reagan candidacy. We also were reminded, and I think the Ford campaign saw a bit of the same thing, that it's always dangerous to assume that what somebody tells you is what he's thinking. A lot of the time what somebody is telling you is an excuse for doing or not doing something. For example, we would often hear from somebody who had just decided that he was going to support Mr. Ford—who had said "yes" to one of Ford's people traveling about the country —and he would say that he would have supported our man but our man was dragging his feet. What he ordinarily meant was that this was the most convenient excuse he could find. I think the Ford people were running into the same problem, particularly in the South, where they would approach people and say, "We'd like you to sign up with the president," and the people would say, "Well, gee, we'd love to, but you've got this guy [Vice President] Rockefeller on the ticket." They weren't really saying that "if you get Rockefeller off the ticket, we'll support the president"; they were using that as an excuse for withholding their support.

I came into the campaign in August 1975, after many of the things that we've already discussed had occurred. I had been on Capitol Hill, and I think that to understand the atmosphere among Republicans, particularly among conservative Republicans, one has to go back to when Mr. Ford became president. At that point there wasn't any great hostility toward Mr. Ford. He was very popular with the general public, and just about everyone that I knew and dealt with wished him well in those days and hoped that it was going to work out. Then, later on, for a variety of reasons, a lot of conservative Republicans began to conclude that the Ford administration was not moving in the kinds of directions that they felt it should move in, and that the president was not getting much of a grip on the popular imagination. It was during that period that there was a lot of third party talk, and an exploration of various alternatives. I was one who felt that the Republican party should continue to be the vehicle through which conservatives should work to achieve their political goals. There were meetings held in various parts of the country at that time, with a lot of discussion centered around the questions of whether there would be a Reagan candidacy, whether there should be one, and if there should be one, how it should develop, and so on.

A couple of things happened during that period that convinced me that a Reagan candidacy could be viable. One was the criticism of Ford during various meetings of conservative members of the Senate. It is interesting that Gerald Ford at his most popular was subject to more criticism from members of the Senate than Richard Nixon had been even when he was in trouble. I think this illustrates the fact that one of the advantages of incumbency in any office is that once you've run and people have supported you, they perceive an attack on you as an attack on them, on their judgment. Mr. Ford had the disadvantage of never having asked people to make any kind of a real psychological commitment to him, and I think that seriously undermined the strength of his incumbency. The second event, which really convinced me, took place in August, after I had decided to join the Reagan campaign, when John Sears and I went to Florida to explore the possibility of putting something together down there. While I had already concluded that this was a worthwhile exercise, I didn't relish the thought of having people whom I knew and liked begin to tear us apart, which is ordinarily what happens when you challenge an incumbent, regardless of the merits of your case. When we got to Florida, we discovered that there were a lot of people who agreed that a challenge would be wise, and a lot of people who disagreed, but there wasn't anyone who was upset about the challenge. Here again was a sign of the lack of psychological commitment that really undermined the strength of the incumbency and made a challenge viable at that point.

ROCKEFELLER WITHDRAWAL

NAUGHTON: David Keene mentioned Nelson Rockefeller, a name somewhat out of the past. What led up to his withdrawal from the ticket [in November 1975], and to what extent was the president a party to that? He certainly didn't seem to discourage it, despite having earlier described Rockefeller as the best qualified man for the job. Was the withdrawal an attempt to appease the conservatives?

TEETER: I think that President Ford believed, when he originally selected Rockefeller, that he was the best man for the job. I think that he still has great respect for him, that in many ways he would have liked to have kept him on the ticket, that they are very close personally and have a great deal of respect for each other, and I am not clear on the details of why the vice president decided not to continue on the ticket. I do think that more of that decision came from Rockefeller himself than is generally accepted.

NAUGHTON: But it was clearly not a unilateral decision, even though Rockefeller may have made it. Bo Callaway [President Ford Committee chairman] said he was getting word from Republicans across the South and other parts of the country that Rockefeller was very unpopular, and [Secretary of State] Kissinger was also. Why let one go and make no effort to stop him, seemingly, and continue with the other?

TEETER: I don't know the answer to that.

JAMES M. PERRY (columnist, *National Observer*): Didn't both Ford and Reagan polls show what kind of division there was among Republicans on the direction of the Ford administration, and about Rockefeller?

TEETER: I don't think that there was a sharp ideological division in the beginning between Reagan and Ford. The great majority of Republicans are people who just tend to support the Republican ticket one way or the other. The hard core committed people are a relatively small minority of the party. To the regulars, the people who attend the convention and participate in the primaries, there wasn't as much difference as you might think between the president and Governor Reagan in the very beginning. There was some antagonism toward Rockefeller, but I never found it in the polling data to be as strong as some organizational people thought it was.

WIRTHLIN: We didn't find great antagonism toward Rockefeller among the Republican rank and file. Most expressed antagonism was a reflection of those vocal activists who were talking to Callaway and others about the liability of having Rockefeller associated with the president.

TEETER: I don't know the details of the conversations that caused Rockefeller to take himself out of the running, but I do think you have to assume, since Bo Callaway was the manager then, that Bo Callaway was not necessarily unhappy at that decision.

KEENE: If we assume that there was some political reason for Mr. Rockefeller's leaving the ticket, I suggest the reason was that the White House and the Ford campaign perceived the Reagan challenge as almost a purely ideological challenge to the president. But if the challenge was not purely ideological, and we [Reagan people] did not think it was, then getting rid of Nelson Rockefeller would not have appreciably added to the president's support in spite of Mr. Callaway's feelings to the contrary. In my view, the Reagan challenge was a challenge to the president's ability to represent the party, to present an image of leadership, to present himself as the kind of candidate the party wanted. It was, in short, far more than a simple ideological challenge.

SEARS: I agree with that. Though we [Reagan people] certainly did not know why certain things were being done at the White House, we thought that they believed that Reagan's challenge was purely ideological, and so we could try to get them to react about a few things. But even without our assistance, they began to react in ways that we could not predict. The whole business about Rockefeller was entirely a phantom in the minds of some group of people. It was not identified with us. Our view of all the discussion going on about whether Rockefeller was good or bad on the ticket, about whether he should get off, was that politicians were making use of a convenient excuse to tell Mr. Ford's people that they didn't want to support him right then. We first felt that Ford's people must understand this and therefore wouldn't react to it too much, but it seemed that they didn't. Far from solving anything for them, the Rockefeller change, and then some other things that happened, served only to give people the idea that maybe there was something wrong with Mr. Ford's leadership, because he kept reacting to the challenger at the same time [that] he kept trying to ignore him. Many of the moves that the president was making helped us a great deal by improving the credibility of what we were up to.

JOHN D. DEARDOURFF (media consultant for Ford): As to the Rockefeller question, I don't have any particular information, but it seems to me that there were probably two explanations for why he did what he did when he did it. One reason might have been the very bitter lingering memory of what he felt to be abuse in 1964 and an unwillingness to go through that again; also a lack of desire to be vice president again could have been a major factor. But I suspect that there was also a substantial element of gamesmanship involved. There have always been people around Rockefeller who have clung to the idea that he would be a candidate again someday, and I think they probably concocted some very peculiar scenario by which he would get out at that early point and then reemerge into the race sometime later when Reagan had dismembered the president. I agree that there was an overreaction on the part of the president's people to some Republican politicians' unwillingness to commit themselves immediately. Particularly when you have inexperienced people like Callaway, it's easy to misread those signals and to think that you have to do something immediately, to take some fairly dramatic action. Callaway stumbled into the attack on Rockefeller, and that triggered off a whole chain of events.

One point that I want to make for the historical record: there was an incipient candidacy for the presidency immediately after the 1972 elections, and that was [Illinois] Senator Percy's. It never went anywhere, but it's worth pointing out that he believed it would. He was flushed with a big victory in Illinois in 1972, where he had carried every county, had won 50 percent of the black vote, and had been endorsed by the United Auto Workers—a lot of things that are rare for a Republican. He undertook a major planning effort, and that's all it ever became. When Nixon resigned and Ford became president, the whole thing just collapsed. But in terms of the long-range planning of political activity at the presidential level, I think there was something interesting about that.

The one other comment that I have relates to the question of how helpful the Reagan candidacy was. In the absence of that candidacy, I suspect that the Ford campaign never would have gotten itself together, and so in that sense you can argue that it was a necessity. On the other hand, I think that it had two very unfortunate results. First, it continued to focus public attention on the question of how far to the right the Republican party was, whether it was only as far right as President Ford or whether it was prepared to go even further. But then beyond this, the Reagan candidacy also affected the paralysis that existed on the part of the Ford people—maybe the president himself, but certainly the staff—right through the nomination, which all led to the indecision and then to the decision about the vice president. To me, the worse effect of the Reagan candidacy in terms of the general election was that the Ford people believed that their hands were tied in terms of who could be chosen as a running mate. They may have been mistaken on this, but I think the mistake grew out of their earlier fear of the power of the Reagan campaign.

CHARLES S. SNIDER (campaign director for Wallace): We Democrats were strictly on the outside looking in, but I may have a little light to shed on the Rockefeller situation. One of the things that kept popping up in our polling, especially among independents, was a relating of Rockefeller to tax-free foundations. Governor Wallace had been effective in getting people to see a connection with their higher taxes. And, of course, this was one of the key issues—high taxes and inflation. We discussed and maybe had bets going on whether the Ford people would dump both Vice President Rockefeller and Secretary of State Kissinger in an effort to corral the independent vote that was out there, which we were losing and Governor Reagan was picking up. The independent vote could be the difference in the nomination, and both Rockefeller and Kissinger were highly disliked by the independents as a whole.

REAGAN PRIMARY STRATEGY

NAUGHTON: It's been said that in the White House there was no strategy for the primaries, and in the Reagan campaign there was a slightly erratic strategy. I'd like to hear about what went into the Reagan strategy for the primaries, and whether, as it seemed, they intended to knock the president out rather quickly.

SEARS: We [Reagan people] would have liked to have done that, and I think we would have if we had won in New Hampshire. But the whole business of organizing yourself for a presidential campaign these days has to start with an understanding of the new campaign finance law,* which among other things is an incumbent bill. It was not passed to be that, but it certainly is, in my view. The existence of the law has changed a great deal about the conduct of presidential nomination politics. I think in this past year, perhaps in our case but certainly on the Democratic side, it may well have determined who obtained the nominations. A second factor that needs to be understood is the existence today of thirty primaries, which is far more than the Republicans had the last time they had a contested race for the nomination. When you try to decide how you're going to run thirty primary races on $10 million, and run against an incumbent, it gets very involved, to say the least. The first thing you realize is that it's just impossible. That leaves you to decide how you may achieve some momentum out of winning in some particular primaries, and how that momentum and the publicity surrounding it can be used to carry you throughout the other states where your funding is not going to be adequate to the job.

We very quickly came to the belief that if we were going to run a campaign, we really had little alternative but to focus very directly on New Hampshire. The quicker we could deliver a telling blow to the incumbent, the better. Indeed, the way that we could justify ourselves in a race that most people thought was impossible would be to defeat him someplace, the earlier the better. Many people looked at Reagan as a presidential candidate and thought his support was lim-

*The 1974 law included the following provisions. To qualify for up to $5 million in matching federal grants, candidates for a major party presidential nomination are each required to raise $5,000 in each of twenty states in amounts of $250 or less, and are then limited in spending to the total of $10 million. (With money allowed for fundraising expenses and two cost-of-living increases, this turned out to be $13.1 million per candidate.) The nominees of major parties are entitled to approximately $22 million each from the treasury for the general election, and are prohibited from raising or spending additional funds. Individuals cannot contribute more than $1,000 in each nomination and election contest, and are restricted to giving no more than $25,000 a year to all federal candidates. The major political parties are provided $2 million in federal grants for convention support, and are restricted to a ceiling of $3.2 million on the amount they can spend on the general election campaign raised from private contributions. Disclosure requirements apply to all gifts of $100 or above, as well as to all expenditures. The Federal Election Commission was established to supervise disclosure, make advisory opinions, and issue regulations.

The Supreme Court decision of January 30, 1976, required that all the members of the Federal Election Commission must be presidential appointees. It held that expenditure limitations were not constitutional, but that presidential candidates who accepted public financing could be held to them. Congress passed various amendments to the 1974 act, which conformed to the Court decision, on May 4. The president signed them into law on May 11, 1976, freeing over $2 million in federal matching funds that had been held up since the suspension on March 20, the Court's deadline for congressional action.

ited to the South and existed really nowhere else, with the possible exception of California, and it was important to us to dispel that idea. A win in New Hampshire was very important to us, given the fact that, limited to $10 million, it was impossible for us to carry on an active campaign in all of the primaries.

As a challenger, you discover that many things are less expensive for an incumbent. When you're running against an incumbent, for example, you have to realize that the regular party apparatus in most states will support him. This does not necessarily mean that the party people prefer him over your candidate, but as a matter of order and custom in politics, they will support him. So the incumbent saves a great deal of money because he doesn't have to go out and manufacture an organization. In many instances, the regular party headquarters can be used as the incumbent's headquarters, whereas you have a different problem locating yours. You look at a large state like New York, for instance, where the vast majority of the county chairmen were in a position where they had to support Mr. Ford. When you look at New York and you total up the bill of what it might cost you to go in there, you have to estimate a bill that might well put a crimp in your ability to go anyplace else. And even then, you might not even achieve parity with the person you are running against.

Had we won in New Hampshire and thus created a momentum, we might have entered a few other primaries. But we did not feel that we were necessarily losing anything by not entering New York [April 6] and Pennsylvania [April 27]. We felt that we probably, by means of the bargaining process, could derive as many delegates as we might have elected by spending a lot of money. I think in New York's case that proved to be true, though I'm less sure about Pennsylvania. While it is true that our strategy did look a little erratic, it was dictated by the economics of the situation as well as by the political realities. If we had won in New Hampshire, I think we would have won in Florida [March 9] and then in Illinois [March 16]. The week before the New Hampshire primary, our polling showed us ahead in Florida; then on the Saturday after the New Hampshire primary, the poll showed us eighteen points down, which gives you some idea of what momentum—or lack of it—can do.

NAUGHTON: But Gene McCarthy developed a momentum in 1968 out of a showing considerably poorer in New Hampshire, and almost defeated the incumbent president. Can you shed some light on why it was that the Reagan campaign, unlike McCarthy's, did slump after New Hampshire?

SEARS: Most of the people who are here, whichever race they've been in, would, I think, agree on one thing—that what happens matters less than the perception about what happens. Even though we came closer than anybody else to winning the New Hampshire primary over a sitting president, we were perceived as having lost it. One of the reasons for this was that we were perceived during December, January, and February as having a better organization in New Hampshire than Mr. Ford did. I think we did, too, but this fact led a lot of people to believe that we could win the race very easily. People could see that we were doing things, and they could not see the same things on another side. They would go around with Reagan and see that his crowds were enthusiastic and quite large in comparison to previous years. People felt that we had managed to put together an organization in New Hampshire that was broad enough to attract voters from the moderate as well as the conservative sections of the party. All this led people to believe before the primary was run that if we didn't win it at that point, then we were losers, regardless of how close we might come and regardless of how our performance might stack up against other people's in previous years.

NOFZIGER: Toward the end of that campaign, the press perceived Reagan as a winner, and when he didn't win, the natural assumption was that he was a loser. In addition, our people traveling with Reagan up there, with the exception of Hugh Gregg [Reagan's New Hampshire campaign chairman], were looking toward a victory and were optimistic, and that optimism came through in their individual dealings with the press. The day after the election, the letdown on that airplane and elsewhere was so noticeable that the traveling press perceived the Reagan people as having viewed it as a loss. That naturally added to their own perception of it as a loss.

KEENE: There was a general feeling, not only in our traveling party but among the rest of us, that we [Reagan people] were ahead. A lot of our people up there said we were in good shape, and most of the people in the press said that we were in good shape. After going up there for primary night, I rode back with a reporter who said, "You have just committed an unpardonable sin. You have just managed to prove all of us wrong. What am I supposed to write now? I could have written a hundred pages about why Ronald Reagan won the New Hampshire primary. What am I supposed to do now, write 'Gerald Ford won today because he's President'?" The general letdown had a snowballing effect that we had no way of stopping. We knew that this would occur if we lost, and maybe that's why we had such long faces afterward.

WIRTHLIN: The $90 billion speech* also cost Reagan momentum. It put the governor on the defensive so much that he was not able to play completely by his own game plan. Some have said that the Reagan strategy appeared erratic. I think it was really two-tiered, rather than erratic. The first tier was heavily based upon developing momentum out of New Hampshire. I was skeptical of that initially, because I had read all of the classic academic papers which say that the bandwagon effect doesn't exist. But then we did some very careful analysis of the impact of the New Hampshire primary on past elections, particularly on the Democratic side, and found that we could expect either a gain or a loss of about fifteen to eighteen percentage points in the primaries following. I turned from being a skeptic to being a strong supporter of the momentum hypothesis. In New Hampshire, Reagan ran 8 percent ahead during January, but that lead eroded when the president came into the state, and we found ourselves behind going into the last ten days. Then the governor recovered somewhat and pulled it back up—and this was then reflected in the election itself. The second tier of the strategy was to make a strong showing in Florida [March 9], North Carolina [March 23], and Texas [May 1] regardless of the New Hampshire outcome.

ALAN L. OTTEN (correspondent, Wall Street Journal): Other than lack of leadership, what were the issues you thought were going to give Reagan the nomination?

SEARS: In New Hampshire, the real issue was leadership. But saying negative things about Mr. Ford was a risky business in New Hampshire, where about a third of the people call themselves conservatives, and about another third moderates. With that kind of mix in the electorate, it did not appear that we would make hay for ourselves by taking on the president directly. While people might have a certain lack of confidence in his leadership, a direct attack on him might raise the charge that you were dividing the party and hitting a nice guy who, though not as good as he should be, deserved a little compassion. This would have reinforced the view that perhaps Reagan was too stringent, too right wing, and too narrow a candidate to be

---

*Candidate Reagan proposed that about $90 billion in federal programs (in such areas as welfare, education, and housing) be gradually transferred to the states, which would then determine their future design and scope.

president. If we had won in New Hampshire, I think we might have taken a little stronger position by the time we got to Florida, simply because the voter attitudes there were different. In Florida there was strong feeling that our national defense posture was not adequate, and that detente had not been as successful a program as people had thought. It was in our own interest, regardless of the outcome in New Hampshire, to begin to hit those issues harder when the New Hampshire primary was over.

There's one more thing to mention about the period between the end of December and the actual running of the primary in New Hampshire. We had been noticing for most of 1975 that people's perceptions about what was going to happen in the country were very pessimistic, and of course, that's bad news for the incumbent. But we began to notice in December and January that among Republicans, though not among Democrats or independents, attitudes began to be more optimistic. This change, as much as anything else, accounted for our loss of some support.

One more thing: I've always believed that weather doesn't have much to do with anything, but I can recall getting off the plane on primary day and noticing that it was some ungodly temperature for that time of year in New Hampshire—like forty degrees—and the sun was out. And I found out that evening that more people than expected had voted that day. Even though the race itself was very close, we felt that, with our superior organization, we could deliver the votes that were there for us. Usually, if your organization in a primary is better than the other fellow's, that's worth a point or two. What actually happened in New Hampshire, though, was that a lot of people voted on their own, without benefit of organizational help. We thought approximately 100,000 people would vote; actually, about 110,000 people voted. I strongly suspect that the extra 10,000 people, who had indicated in the polls earlier that they had little interest in actually voting, mostly voted for the incumbent. Also, because the Democratic race was not attracting a great deal of interest, we got every bit of attention around, and that probably encouraged more people to vote.

BEN J. WATTENBERG (adviser to Jackson): Was there a sense in the New Hampshire campaign, as there was in other campaigns later on in that year, that Reagan was badly used by the press? If so, do you feel that there was an ideological component?

SEARS: I don't think that we were mistreated by the press in New Hampshire. The press was, perhaps, reacting to perceptions that pre-

dated the actual running of the primary. But you can question yourself constantly about what is perception and what is fact, and what
responsibility people have to recognize fact as opposed to perception. In politics you reach a point where such distinctions are not
possible—not for the press, not for the politicians. Sometimes perceptions are going to help you, and sometimes they'll hurt you. It
did us no harm to go to New Hampshire—the impression was created
there that we had a credible and serious candidate. This at least
helped us. Things never quite evened out there, of course, but there
are times when you're helped, and times when you're hurt. That's
just one of the facts of being in the business.

FORD PRIMARY STRATEGY

NAUGHTON: The White House certainly used the perception that
the president had the momentum all the way to the North Carolina
primary. Signals were even being sent that it had been a good fight,
and that maybe Governor Reagan would like to join forces and end
it. Was there a strategy in the Ford campaign other than to enter all
the primaries? And how was the momentum lost?

TEETER: There are two or three things you have to think about in
terms of the president's primary campaign, and, for that matter, his
campaign before the primaries. First of all, Gerald Ford had never
run in a statewide race in his life, and probably the last seriously contested race he had run in was the Republican primary in 1948. He
was a very inexperienced politician in that sense. He had been in congressional races fighting the Democrats in a very traditional partisan
way for a long time, but I don't think he had any feel whatsoever
about how to run against another Republican, particularly against
someone coming at him from the direction that Reagan was. For instance, in Florida, our data showed that people thought he was too
soft on national defense, whereas he had spent twenty-five years on
the Armed Services Committee believing that he was one of the
toughest people in the country on national defense. To add to this,
there was not an overwhelming amount of political experience on the
White House staff. No one in the White House, including the president, really had developed any kind of idea of who his constituency
was and who it ought to be in either the general election or the primaries. Who were the 51 percent of the people who were going to get
him elected? He was the first president ever who had never been
through the general election process, where he had to think about
who his constituency was and what his strategy should be.

The president was unknown. Even though he had been president for a year and a half or two years, there were a great many people who really didn't know very much about him at all: most of the people knew he was from Michigan and that he was a congressman, but very few people, for instance, even knew that he was a lawyer. They didn't have much of a view of whether he was a liberal, a moderate, or a conservative. The perceptions that were held about the president were held very thinly. There was no strong psychological commitment to the president, either in the general election electorate or among the primary electorate, and this ultimately caused all the problems we had in the primaries. A great number of people were "soft," had a very thin attachment to the president, and were undecided.

Since neither an issue nor a constituency strategy had been developed, the Reagan candidacy did have a positive effect in that it forced the Ford campaign into so much trouble that we had to develop a better managed organizational structure. But I think that the Reagan candidacy may also have been harmful. The Reagan candidacy kept the president from developing his strategy and from doing things that might appeal to a general election constituency; at the same time, the fact that he was president and had to govern kept him from going directly after some of the Reagan constituency. This left him in an indecisive state, which was heightened by the budget situation. At the time of the State of the Union in 1975, we discussed all kinds of proposals, many of which he seriously thought about doing. But he had several budget constraints, primarily in the domestic policy area; the budget was a very serious constraint, for instance, in the area of health care. The president proposed in the State of the Union address that we go into a health insurance program for catastrophic illness. The fact is that the cost of that kind of insurance program is not overwhelming, but budget considerations limited his proposal to people over sixty-five, whereas he might otherwise have gone with a broader coverage.

As for our strategy in the primaries, that was pretty well set out for us in the president's announcements; he said he was entering all the primaries, so we didn't spend much time deliberating that. But once he had said that, our problem with the $10 million limit was tremendous. While there may be some things that are cheaper for an incumbent than a challenger, campaigning is not one of them. The cost of moving an incumbent president is fantastic, particularly when you are being scrupulous. On the other hand, there are some things that an incumbent benefits greatly from—like press coverage, White House staff.

NAUGHTON: But obviously a president doesn't need to do as much campaigning out on the road as a challenger does.

TEETER: For all candidates on both sides, the campaign spending limit does decrease the ability to organize a large number of states. You simply cannot put together a political organization in a significant proportion of thirty states with $10 million. I suspect that every campaign will agree that it is just impossible. Given the fact that we were committed to enter all the primaries, the strategy going into the early primaries was to win in New Hampshire and then continue winning the next two or three or five, whatever it might take to get Reagan out of the race. Or even if he didn't withdraw, he would be rendered a much less formidable candidate. We thought we were close to that goal in New Hampshire. I spent a great deal of time talking to people in the White House and on the campaign staff, and talking to reporters themselves, to emphasize that if we won by one vote in New Hampshire, we won, and if we lost by one vote, we lost. This idea that Reagan could get 48 percent or 49 percent and win was just not true in the American system of "winner take all" politics. What allowed me to cultivate this idea successfully was the growing perception that New Hampshire was a Reagan state, with the [Manchester] *Union Leader* and the governor [Meldrim Thomson], and he did have a chance to win. If the first primary had been in Wisconsin or someplace else, then it would have been much tougher for me to convince people that it really was not a victory for Reagan if he got 40 or 45 percent.

One thing we thought would help us, and I think it did, was that Republican regulars don't like primaries or intraparty fights. Given that, they would tend to support the incumbent, when they had to make that decision in the last day or two. We were also helped by the $90 billion proposal: it gave our people something to talk about.

REAGAN CONTINGENCY STRATEGY

MARK A. SIEGEL (executive director, Democratic National Committee): When the Reagan campaign was formulated, presumably creating as many options as possible, why didn't you file reasonable delegates in states like New Jersey, Ohio, Illinois, and Pennsylvania, where there are early filing dates for late primaries? Then if you had wanted to make major races in those states, at least you could have done it. I know your primary strategy was to wipe Ford out early on, but wasn't there a contingency strategy that assumed [that] you might have to go down to the wire fighting for every single delegate?

SEARS: As for New York, we made a determination quite a bit prior to the New Hampshire primary to leave it alone. The New York county chairmen had met in the fall of 1975 and had decided that, contrary to their earlier intention to field a slate of Ford delegates as an organizational matter, they would field a slate of uncommitted delegates. This happened to be right after Governor Rockefeller decided not to be vice president any longer. As long as nobody was committed on that slate and we could talk to local leaders, as we did later on, we did not feel that our chances would be hurt in the end.

As for Pennsylvania, some of the same things pertained, because Pennsylvania also fielded a slate of uncommitted delegates. We felt that if we were doing well otherwise, we could deal in various places for delegates—just on the basis that a slate that does not have a governor is not entirely controllable. Looking at 1968 in comparison, there were governors in both New York and Pennsylvania. We managed to get four delegates [for Nixon] out of New York in 1968 only because four people with enough local clout happened to run against the organization slate and win. In Pennsylvania, the favorite son candidate there, Governor Shafer, held that posture for too long; by virtue of that, we were able to get in underneath and bargain for eventually twenty delegates. But the prospect of running slates against uncommitted slates has not been appealing.

As for Ohio, we came very close to missing the deadline. We ended up with slates in all of the districts that we thought we had a chance of carrying. We never thought that we would be able to carry the whole state, largely because of the amount of money that we were going to have to spend in May at a time when we projected our funds would be low. The filing deadline in Ohio was a couple of days after the North Carolina primary. At that point, to be honest about our contingency or otherwise plans, there was not a great deal of consideration being given to running in Ohio. More consideration was being given to paying the hotel bills.

PAYING THE BILLS

Looking ahead, it was possible to see a given day in June [June 8] when we'd be running in the California primary, the Ohio primary, and the New Jersey primary, all of which would require a great deal of money. Given our financial situation, and realizing that we definitely would have to do well in California to maintain our race, it looked like the better part of valor to make some contacts inside the New Jersey organization in order to have something to do with what kinds of delegates the organization fielded, and then to take our chances. Not only in terms of the money was all this staggering but also in terms of the difficulty of being able to campaign in New Jersey at the same time we were going to have to campaign in California. In April, we still had not won the Texas primary, which is the point at which most people began to feel that we might have a chance of getting nominated. The North Carolina event had been an interesting phenomenon to a lot of people and created interest in what might happen in May, but until we won in Texas, and indeed until we followed up that win with some victories on the following Tuesday, most people did not feel that the Reagan race was going to be significant. This was another question related to the campaign finance laws—whether we could raise any significant money from April on had to be taken into account. So what we did was to protect our interests as well as we could and try to isolate the funds that we had available to create the momentum to win.

We were really financially strapped in May, even though things were better than they had been in March or April. We won very strongly in Texas, and on the following Tuesday [May 4], we won in Indiana, Georgia, and Alabama, and lost only three districts in Indiana. The Indiana victory was very significant to us because it showed us that we could win in a Midwestern state that was historically a Republican state. We followed that up by winning in Nebraska [May 11], which created some more good perceptions for us, and we reached a point where people were thinking we should do very well in the state of Michigan [May 18]. Governor Wallace had pulled 100,000 votes in Michigan three years before, and some people felt that automatically all those votes would go to us. We didn't get them, I don't think Mr. Udall got them, it didn't look as though Mr. Carter got them because he was in a close race with Mr. Udall, but there is a great deal of evidence to suggest that Mr. Ford got them. Looking back at the circumstances in 1972, we realized that there was no Republican race going on that year, and that what evidently happened was that a lot of Republicans voted for Mr. Wallace, for whatever reason. After we didn't do well in the Michigan primary, our momentum slowed again; the outcome of the Michigan primary did more to harm us right then than the fact that we didn't pull a great vote and the fact that we had been perceived to be going to do a lot better than that.

NAUGHTON: Could you briefly describe how serious the money problems were, and what effect the pause in the federal funding had on the Reagan campaign?

SEARS: Things were pretty critical. All of the people who had done business with us would ultimately be paid, but nobody knew exactly when, and technically under the law it's very difficult to get credit anyway. As I recall, in March we had unpaid bills that amounted to about $1.5 million. We were not raising a great deal of money, and so the situation, if nothing happened, was bound to get progressively worse. This led to the idea that Mr. Reagan should go on television, and that was quite successful. We raised about $1.3 million for an expense of a little less than $200,000. And once the mechanism was established, a great deal of the money was matchable, upwards of 80 percent. According to the new campaign finance law, the money comes in as you are able to prove that you're entitled to it; and then after you prove that, there's another four week period before you actually get it. So all through the month of May, we were still receiving matching funds from that original television show. It kept going week to week as we ran three or four primaries. Once the primaries dropped off and thus most of our expenses, and we were receiving more money from fundraising because we were doing well, we had very little to spend the money on. Then the really ridiculous thing happened: people kept sending us money, and we couldn't use it because it was over the overall limit.

NOFZIGER: I think John [Sears] is minimizing what the predicament actually was. When we first said we were going to go on television, lo and behold, we didn't have the money to buy the time. When we finally scraped up the $86,000 to buy the time, we discovered we didn't have the money for the production costs. We finally scraped that up on a desperate day, with the people actually waiting on overtime for us to give them the money so that they could proceed with the production. Then we came into California. We eventually got a lot of money during the last three weeks in California, but I'm sitting there in early May, and they are sending me about $5,000 a week to try to run the state of California. All this means is that under this new law, whoever attempts to run against an incumbent is going to have to plan very carefully where his money goes. There's no way you can put it into primaries and at the same time try to put together something in the other states.

JOHN B. GABUSI (campaign director for Udall): Until the end, was there any time when you didn't feel the financial pressures in your campaign?

SEARS: The pressures went right up through the convention. We kept cutting down on our convention budget because our comptroller was saying, "Hey, we've got expenses coming in and so forth, and here are our projections."

TEETER: As we [Ford people] moved toward the convention, it was also partly a problem of exceeding the limit, because you can't predict what all the expenses are going to be. As the primaries happen, and you have to judge your strategies, there is no way of predicting how long you're going to have to go in the primaries and what your expenses are going to be. Particularly in the Republican case, you came up against the need to run the campaign all the way up until the middle of August [and the convention], all within the same limit.

CLOSING PRIMARIES

NAUGHTON: In North Carolina both sides seemed to be surprised by the outcome, and some changes seemed to occur thereafter. Reagan went on television and began campaigning more aggressively; the president took on his second campaign chairman [Rogers C.B. Morton] and began spending more time using the White House. What happened in the period of the closing primaries and the delegate hunt that changed the complexity of the race?

TEETER: North Carolina changed it immensely, and then things began to snowball. Many of the primaries followed exactly the same pattern: the president would start substantially ahead, and that would hold until Reagan went into the state to campaign. At one point we [Ford people] thought we had a substantial lead in North Carolina, and decided not to incur the cost of doing another poll closer to the election, or of sending the president in during the last week or so of the campaign. There is no guarantee that either move would have changed the result, of course, but I think the decisions were based on political inexperience. After North Carolina we got into a series of losses in Texas, Indiana, Alabama, Nebraska, and a couple of other Southern primaries, and then it was more of a contest than it had been even right before New Hampshire.

SIEGEL: It seemed very clear a week or ten days before the June 8 primary that Governor Reagan was very substantially ahead in California. What kept him campaigning in California, where he knew he was going to win, rather than in other parts of the country, in view of the fact that every delegate counted so much?

NOFZIGER: We had decided that the governor would campaign in California during the last eight days. As we came toward the end, I informed our people in Washington that we were in good shape, so they took him for a day and a half and put him in Ohio. All the same, with less than two weeks to go, our tracking polls showed that President Ford was closing, and we came down to one night when we were dead even. Our perception that the governor was well ahead was not being borne out by the polls. We didn't seem to have any momentum in California until the last ten days, and then the governor came in and campaigned in his own state. The Ford people tried at the last minute to change the law from a "winner take all" situation to a proportionate one and got caught at it, and they also came out with an ad saying that Governor Reagan couldn't start a war but President Reagan could—and that also reacted against them quite severely. At the tail end of it, we had some things going that we didn't have two weeks before.

WIRTHLIN: Governor Reagan generally holds his Republicans extremely well in California, but our polls were beginning to show that the president was being viewed there as the winner, and there was some slippage. But the Ford ad that Lyn Nofziger mentioned turned it around and added as much as four or five percentage points to the Reagan win. We found out about the ad on a Saturday morning, we polled Saturday afternoon, and by that evening we knew that even 45 percent of the Ford supporters and an overwhelming majority of the undecideds felt the ad was unfair and unjustified. We cut a radio ad that said, in essence, "This is an advertisement for Governor Reagan, but it's a different kind of ad because what we're going to ask you to do is go out of your way to listen to the President Ford Committee ad. We think that it tells you more about the President Ford Committee than it does about Ronald Reagan." And that, I think, added about four or five percentage points on top of our support.

NAUGHTON: Is there any measure of what kind of reaction there was outside of Reagan's home state, even though the ad didn't run elsewhere?

WIRTHLIN: None that we picked up. It appeared to have impacted only on the California race.

DEARDOURFF: It was my impression during the entire course of the primaries that there was an ability of voters in a given state to tune in and out depending on whether the primary was being held in that state at that time or not. I think it worked to the advantage of the Carter candidacy that he was able to say different things in different places because people really didn't pay much attention; and even though the national media somehow thought they were communicating, I don't think people were listening. That's why I don't think you could find ten people outside California who would have an opinion about that ad.

CAMPAIGN ISSUES

WATTENBERG: Watching from the outside, I felt that the Reagan campaign started very much on domestic issues and finished in August with morality and foreign policy. If you look at public opinion polls, there was a sharp shift in 1975 and 1976 toward a hard position on foreign policy. The year 1975 was the year of the Mayaguez incident and of Solzhenitsyn and of [Defense Secretary] Schlesinger's firing and of [Ambassador] Moynihan's appearances at the United Nations. I had the sense that the Reagan campaign caught fire when it became very oriented toward foreign policy through the issue of the Panama Canal, which I thought was a code name for a series of other foreign policy issues.

SEARS: Because of the troubles in the economy in 1975, there was an attitude of pessimism in this country. Reagan was the first to get into the business of running against the establishment in Washington, and then Mr. Carter got into it at the time of the caucus in Iowa [January 19] and hit it even harder. It was not as valuable an issue for us into 1976 because Republicans were changing their attitude about it, though Democrats were not. Mr. Carter was able to keep to that issue, whereas we drifted into the foreign policy field.

WIRTHLIN: When people judged the president on his performance in the foreign policy area generally, he got very high marks—higher than those he received for the way he handled, for example, unemployment, inflation, energy, and a wide variety of domestic issues. But when we broke attitudes down on specifics—on detente, on the Panama Canal, somewhat on Kissinger—we found sharp criticism of the president, particularly among Republican activists. Right from the beginning, Reagan was perceived not only by Republicans but also by Democrats and independents as being stronger, more competent, and more decisive than the president. With the loss in New Hampshire we [Reagan people] felt that we had to confront very directly the issue of Ford's leadership style, and the issues best suited to highlighting differences in leadership style were in the area of foreign policy, but couched in very, very specific and precise terms. The shift to the specific foreign policy issues came after the New Hampshire loss, in the Florida campaign. The press—either NBC or CBS—indicated that Reagan's foreign policy thrust had failed because we lost Florida. The thing they didn't know was that right after the New Hampshire primary, we were down eighteen percentage points there, and that we made up about fourteen of those percentage points in ten days using the foreign policy issues as the vehicle to contrast leadership style. We continued to run with this, and it finally paid off in North Carolina. Then the stage was set for Texas, where every element was just right to bring home that big victory.

SELECTION OF SCHWEIKER

NAUGHTON: Did Reagan then throw it away with the selection of Senator Richard Schweiker [as his running mate]?

KEENE: I don't think that the Schweiker decision [announced July 26] hurt us at all. It came at a point when it appeared that we were in deep trouble. Once the primaries and the state conventions were over, once all the delegates had been selected and we were still behind, there were a lot of people out there who wouldn't say they were for us but were talking like they might go for us under the right circumstances. We came into a period when the advantages that the president had were almost insurmountable. It was pretty tough to overcome the fact that he could zero in on convention delegate Mrs. Jones and bring her into the Oval Office and impress the hell out of her and get that commitment. There were signs throughout our operation not only that some of the uncommitted were moving as a result of this wooing, but that our own people were beginning to crack. I thought that unless we did something, we had a week at most. The Schweiker selection had merit beyond this, but it also kept us alive and kept the race going right on to the end. It didn't work, but it did come close to working; it threw everything up in the air and allowed us to maneuver around a little bit more. In terms of the situation we faced, I think it was successful.

SEARS: The thing about our circumstances was that any time we [Reagan people] weren't carrying the game, we were probably in trouble whether we knew it or not; whenever we were caught flat-footed, we were going to get killed by the power that was always there to deal with us. Of course, the White House had to operate with a much larger bureaucracy to make its decisions (which is one of the nice things about being on the outside), and so decisions couldn't be made so quickly. Also, we could force reactions from the White House because incumbents and people around them fear embarrassment of some sort when they often ought just to ignore things. But the important thing was this: there were a number of people, enough people to get us nominated, who would keep telling us that yes, they would be for us, but they couldn't do it right now. This always reminded me of something I had read in the *Confessions of Saint Augustine*, where he remembers in his youth praying to God, "God, give me chastity, but please not now." Whatever they believed at the time we asked them, by the time of the convention [August 16] they weren't really going to go for us. What we direly needed was some way to carry the fight, and to get some maneuverability again. At this particular juncture, the perception was growing that if things stayed as they were, we were going to get counted out of the race; and if that perception continued to grow, we couldn't be sure of those people who had already committed to us. The Schweiker decision looked toward running in the fall; and we thought it would give us a very good chance of winning then. It was our feeling that if the Reagan-Schweiker ticket was presented to the country, we would have a united party, and we would have a good chance, in opposition to Mr. Carter, to carry some states in the Northeast. We felt that we would have a good chance of carrying New Jersey with Mr. Schweiker on the ticket, and certainly Pennsylvania, and probably Connecticut. There were many reasons why Mr. Schweiker was selected. I think we might well have wound up selecting him even if we had not had to worry about the nomination.

PERRY: Wasn't there also the fact of Schweiker's friendship with Drew Lewis [Ford chairman in Pennsylvania], and your belief that the Schweiker selection could break out votes for Reagan in Pennsylvania?

SEARS: After the negotiation process was completed, Mr. Schweiker volunteered that he might be able to talk to his friend Mr. Lewis. We had not talked about this prior to that time. I did know that Mr. Lewis had not been getting on too well with some of the Ford organization, and that he was a close friend of Mr. Schweiker. But I was not of the opinion myself that anything was necessarily going to happen. In politics you can have very close friendships, but when people get down to a position, they pretty much have to stay where they are. They would lose their credibility if they were to jump up and move when there had been no appropriate public conditioning. It would destroy their own political futures. Mr. Lewis found himself in a very difficult position upon Mr. Schweiker's being selected, but all that I hoped for was that the selection would require some reevaluation in a few states, and that we could take advantage of that. What surprised me was that, instead of people not being sure for a few days how this would all break down, there was instantaneous reaction that it was a mistake. It was a great surprise, and people in the press and elsewhere don't like to be surprised. Also, people did not really understand our circumstances. I think they would have understood them in another week if we had just let them, but then it would have been too late to select Mr. Schweiker.

PERRY: Did you consider anyone else?

SEARS: We considered everybody in the Senate who was a Republican, people in the House who were Republicans, and all of our governors. We seriously considered these people, and I'll tell you, that didn't take very long. We could kiss off the House because nobody there was well enough known, and if you are running for the presidency out of a convention in late August and have to spend three weeks when you're thirty points behind explaining who the vice president is—that's a little difficult. We could whip through the Senate real fast—a lot of our people in the Senate were just too old. We thought we could throw Mr. Carter off stride if we were to run at him nationwide, something we were capable of and Mr. Ford was probably not. Mr. Reagan was strong in the South, at least enough to breathe fear into the Carter people that he could hold Texas, and Florida, and maybe a few other states. If we selected Mr. Schweiker or somebody from the Middle West or Northeast, we could better our chances of being understood in those areas and take advantage of the weakness Mr. Carter had among Catholic and Jewish voters and rank and file labor. We were definitely strong enough in the Far West so that we didn't need any vice presidential help out there, and also in the farm states. We came down very quickly to the fact that we needed somebody in the Northeast or the Middle West, and we picked through those names rather quickly and found Mr. Schweiker very attractive.

JESSICA TUCHMAN (director of issues and research for Udall): It was the first commandment in Democratic politics this year that it didn't do you any good to get the nomination unless you could win the general election. Listening to the analysis of your thinking during the time you described, when you were trying to hang on for another three days or five days, I find it hard to believe that you were really thinking at all about the general election.

SEARS: It does nobody, including those who work for presidential candidates, any good to waste a year or two years of their lives just so somebody can get nominated and terribly beaten. I presume there are people who look at nominations as entities in and of themselves, but I don't think any of us [in the Reagan campaign] felt that way and I don't think most people did. I'd been through all this with Nixon in 1968, when we constantly had to bear in mind the overall political situation in the Republican party. It would have been very easy for Nixon in 1968 to adopt the Goldwater mantle of 1964 and just get nominated. But we didn't do it that way simply because there was no reason for Nixon to get nominated if he couldn't win the election.

BRODER: I'd like to know how the choice of Schweiker affected the Ford side. Did it have any effect at all in the battle for the uncommitted delegates?

TEETER: It caused those people who were in the Lewis [Pennsylvania] delegation some pain for a short time, but otherwise I think it made it easier in two ways. It made it easier to go to uncommitted delegates and argue that Reagan was not as ideologically pure as they might have thought he was. But more important, there was a growing perception in the press that Reagan had made a mistake and done something a little flaky, a little desperate. We [Ford people] tried as hard as we could to encourage this view, and things started coming back our way a little bit at that point.

SEARS: For about ten days after the Schweiker decision, there was an idea that we [Reagan people] had just killed ourselves, and yet they couldn't come up with enough delegates to count us out of the race. Finally, people realized again that we were going into the convention and nobody knew who was going to be nominated. This was a help to us, because if we hadn't done something and had gone into the convention with everybody perceiving that we were going to lose, then we would have lost. After Schweiker, there was a question in some people's minds about whether Reagan was as much a conservative as they thought he was, but then that began to clear up. And the Schweiker selection did serve a positive purpose for us. We had been getting hit very heavily by indications that if Reagan ever got nominated, the stock market would fall because it would be perceived that he was too narrowly based a candidate to win nationally and that the Northeast would walk away from the party and thus ensure Mr. Carter's election. After we picked Mr. Schweiker, we didn't have to cope with any of that comment. Also we greatly increased our ability to have discussions with people who had indicated that they might be willing to come with us but feared that Mr. Reagan was not serious about running the campaign in the Northeast. It was then too that we began to develop the idea that perhaps Mr. Ford should tell the rest of us who he would run with.

KEENE: I had the marginally uncomfortable task of relating the Schweiker choice to some of our [Reagan's] Southern supporters. If we erred in our assessment of what was going to follow the announcement, it was in underestimating the amount of smoke and overestimating the amount of fire it would generate. We thought we were going to lose more delegates in the South than we actually did, but I don't think that we accurately predicted the rhetorical blowup and the ability of the other side to use that. But when you looked at the uncommitted delegates, most of them weren't conservatives, and I don't think that Schweiker necessarily bothered them too much. Of course, there were some that we lost during that period—three or four delegates who moved from uncommitted to Ford were people who should have been ours. All in all, one of the things we were trying to do was not only to get a person who was going to be a good candidate, but to find one who would help the ticket and help us in a lot of other ways. I was much happier with Dick Schweiker after he was chosen than I was at the time, because, as it turns out, he's a pretty good guy.

SEARS: The Schweiker decision did hurt us in some ways. Some people who had been attracted to us quickly decided that we had blown it with all of our natural supporters, and so they didn't come with us. Had the perception been instead that maybe it was a good move, then we would have picked up a number of votes in New Jersey and Pennsylvania. But in fact the immediate perception was that we had just lost the Mississippi delegation and were losing votes all over the place.

WHITE HOUSE PERSPECTIVE

DUVAL: I'd like to make two observations from the standpoint of the perspective or lack of perspective you have at the White House.

First, there absolutely has to be a strategy for a presidential candidate, and that strategy, at minimum, has to take account of what you stand for and why you want the office, and beyond that, who your constituency is and what it is that you're trying to deal with. You cannot build that strategy while you're in the race; you have to have it before you start. Fortunately, the president did have a general election strategy, which was developed during the primaries in a separate effort. But we [Ford people] did not have a strategy for the primaries.

Secondly, when you're trying to run for the nomination of your party for the presidency, it is a tremendous distraction if you happen to be president. The fact of the matter is that the nation's problems, especially during early 1976 and the spring—the international economic problems and the domestic problems involving the intelligence community and also foreign policy—took an enormous amount of the president's time. Also, in assessing why the president took a specific action that might appear to be political, one should very carefully assess the context in which that decision was made, in terms of what was going on in the rest of the world.

WATTENBERG: Are you saying that after eighteen months in office, President Ford did not have a substantive sense of what he believed in during those primaries?

DUVAL: What I'm saying is that in terms of a strategy for running—why he was running for office, the basic constituency groups that he appealed to and needed and wanted in all states—he had not, in my judgment, thought that through comprehensively before going into the primaries.

NOFZIGER: You say that the president didn't have enough time to campaign because of all his other problems, but certainly early in the general election, there was a decision to keep him in the White House instead of sending him out to campaign. There was talk too that many of the people in the campaign would have liked to have him stay more in the White House during the primaries.

DUVAL: I didn't say that he didn't have enough time "to campaign," or go out on the stump. What I said was that he didn't have enough time "for the campaign" with its strategy and policy decisions—and these are two different things.

REPUBLICAN CONVENTION

BRODER: What were the problems that had to be dealt with if the Republican party was going to survive the Kansas City convention?

MAHE: As is always the case with Republicans, we [in the Republican National Committee] were very much concerned with the technical aspects of the convention and were preoccupied with organization. I felt that the Republican National Committee was making every effort to try to balance out the needs, wishes, and requirements of the Ford and Reagan campaigns. Our situation was tremendously complicated by the fact that our chairman [Mary Louise Smith] chose to run as a Ford delegate rather than as an uncommitted delegate, and this created a lot of anxiety on the part of a lot of people. After that, there was never any real confidence on the part of many people that the committee was making any effort to be fair and impartial. But we did make the effort, and our primary concern was to pull the event off and avoid the kind of things that all of us remembered about the 1972 Democratic convention.

NOFZIGER: Though I had excellent dealings with the convention director, and felt that he bent over backwards to be fair to both sides, still the Ford people managed to get considerably more rooms and tickets. We [Reagan people] got 100 rooms and the Ford people got maybe 400. This may seem silly, but when you're trying to put your people into a convention, it's tough when you don't have enough rooms in which to put your political operators. It's tough when you don't have enough tickets to go around for your people. In addition, every major officer of the committee and every major speaker of the convention was either a Ford delegate or a Ford supporter—the temporary chairman, the permanent chairman, the keynote speaker, the sergeant-at-arms.

BRODER: As far as the Ford people were concerned, was the contest over before Kansas City, or was it something that still had to be won there?

DUVAL: The contest, as far as we were concerned, was winning the general election and that had two steps to it: one, winning the nomination; and two, being able to get a majority in November. I think it is to our credit that we never separated the two elements. We had some people who were working exclusively on getting the nomination, but we tried to maintain a perspective that would allow us to come out of Kansas City in a position to win the general election. That perspective had a lot to do with how we developed our strategy in Kansas City.

Probably the most distinguishing characteristic of the Ford candidacy for the presidency was that he was a man who had never conducted, much less won, a national election. The question of his ability to win was an important problem that we faced both in the general election and in the primaries. So it was especially important that the president should come out of Kansas City looking like a winner. Thus, it mattered very much that we win those procedural votes. The public perception of how the convention was run would clearly be of extreme importance to our position in the polls and our momentum as we started the general campaign. The platform was really a damage-limiting operation, since we didn't see how it could be of much help to us. Of course, it was clear that if our platform was an embarrassment, then that would weaken our position in attacking the Democratic platform in the general election. Also, if there was considerable adverse publicity about that platform, that would have a negative impact on our campaign.

BRODER: Did the Reagan people believe that they were still in the game?

KEENE: We thought we still had an opportunity if we could get something going. There were enough delegates out there, both uncommitted delegates and delegates nominally supporting the president, who had indicated that under some circumstances they would like to vote for Governor Reagan. We felt that we had to convince them that we would have an opportunity to win if they did vote for Reagan, and that's what much of the maneuvering was about.

QUESTION 16C

BRODER: Why did you decide to make your major fight on a procedural issue rather than on a substantive issue of the platform?

KEENE: We didn't believe that a lot of the uncommitted delegates were ideological conservatives, and so we didn't feel that what we were going to have to do to get them should necessarily involve an ideological position. It's always possible to stir things up on an ideological basis, but we felt that the people who agreed with Ronald Reagan on the issues were already with us by and large, and the ones who didn't agree had overriding reasons to go the other way and it was fairly unlikely that we'd get them. Consequently, we believed that the best way to prove our strength was to find something the primary appeal of which was not essentially ideological. We were going to have to show the delegates that we could win, and that the president might not be able to win, and that we were likely to be able to field a stronger ticket in the general election. We settled on the procedural question 16C*—our position on this had some intrinsic merit, and also, if we won our point, the president would have been forced to commit himself to a running mate and thus lose his power to maneuver with delegates from different parts of the country. We felt that on this issue, if we could get enough people with their own reasons to vote along with our people, we'd both show our strength and force the president to make a move that could only cost him something.

We also felt there was merit to reforming the way the vice presidential candidate is selected. There is a fairly broad consensus that there's something wrong with the way it's done now. Prior to selection in the current method, for instance, candidates tend to tell everyone that it's down to him and one other guy, and if he'll just hang on for a while and vote right, he has a good chance of becoming vice president. Obviously, it can be argued that optimal reform doesn't take place under the kinds of conditions we are discussing, but that's a different point.

NOFZIGER: In trying to convince people who were Ford delegates to go with Reagan, we found that a number of them said, "We approve of it in principle, but we don't think we ought to do it here. Let's wait until the next time." There were a number of people whose politics overcame their belief that a change ought to be made.

KEENE: Also, the question of vice presidential selection had been part of the reform fights of 1972. It had been presented by the liberal side of the party, and as a result, many conservatives had opposed it for that reason. When they got to the 1976 convention, they found themselves being asked to support a proposal that resembled something they had opposed for a long time—and they couldn't do it. Some members of the Republican National Committee were in that position.

---

*Reagan people proposed that convention rules be amended (section C of rule 16) to require that each candidate seeking the party's presidential nomination announce a vice.presidential choice in advance of the balloting. If a candidate did not do so, previously committed delegates would be freed of their obligation to vote for that candidate.

NOFZIGER: In all this, we were trying to halt the Ford people's effort to convince our people that if Ford were the nominee, they could have Reagan as vice president.

KEENE: One of the most effective arguments used against 16C was that if it was passed, Mr. Ford wouldn't be able to offer Mr. Reagan the vice presidential nomination.

But often when you review something like the fight over 16C, you ascribe to it more rationality and control than in fact existed. The fact is that we had less flexibility in the issues area than the procedural area, partly because we weren't totally in control of the people who were concerned about some of the issues. We also believed that the president's strategists were not about to get into a fight with us on a platform issue on which most of the delegates were probably on our side, and that included most of the platform issues we might be likely to support. The Ford people weren't anxious for fights on issues. What fights took place happened because there were a lot of delegates who cared about the issues and fought for them. Some of our people would have done that whether or not we asked them to— in many cases they did it, not against our direction, but certainly without our direction.

NOFZIGER: If we had sought to fight on a platform issue, we would probably have had to move further right than we wanted to. And it seemed obvious to us that the Ford people were deliberately caving in on platform issues because they did not want to fight there —for instance, on the abortion issue.

DUVAL: The only issue that we [Ford people] fought on was the Equal Rights Amendment. I'm not convinced that it was a Reagan-Ford fight, but we took a hard line position in favor of ERA and did everything we could to win. We lost it on the first vote, and on a recount vote the next day we won it.

On the abortion question: as the person who had to relay the president's decision on whether to fight or not to fight, I instructed the people who asked that we would not take a position on that issue as to whether or not we wanted a straightforward vote. The reason for that was that the president felt it was an issue of conscience and not the kind of issue on which to have a party vote. He also felt that a majority of Americans in the general election would react strongly and adversely to making the issue a partisan matter.

"MORALITY IN GOVERNMENT" PLANK

WATTENBERG: What about the foreign policy plank that criticized the incumbent secretary of state? I think in any other democracy this would have caused his resignation, yet it was acquiesced to by President Ford's people.

DUVAL: There's no question that the so-called "morality in government" plank* was perceived to have been a slap at President Ford and Secretary Kissinger, and thus perceived to have been a Ford defeat. The fact that it was perceived to have been a defeat made it one to some extent, but it may be helpful to take a look at the facts, which are quite different from the perceptions. I had specific instructions from the president that we were to fight any plank that would violate certain basic foreign policy objectives. He would not support any position contrary to U.S. foreign policy on, for example, Cuba, Panama, Formosa, Rhodesia, or South Africa. As it turned out, we won every one of those votes, mostly on tie votes at the subcommittee level. We got a platform that reflected administration policy right down the line on the key controversial issues. The "morality in government" paragraph was submitted as preamble language to a section, not really part of the platform, and there was not a word in it that was inconsistent with U.S. policy. But unfortunately, it was interpreted as being a slap at the Ford administration, and we had to decide whether to oppose it. There was no committee vote on it—it was added as an amendment afterwards—so the first place that we had an opportunity to oppose it was on the convention floor.

That vote came up right after the vote on 16C, which was the vote that signaled that the president had won the nomination. It was as if

*From the 1976 Republican platform: "The goal of Republican foreign policy is the achievement of liberty under law and a just and lasting peace in the world. The principles by which we act to achieve peace and to protect the interests of the United States must merit the restored confidence of our people. We recognize and commend that great beacon of human courage and morality, Alexander Solzhenitsyn, for his compelling message that we must face the world with no illusions about the nature of tyranny. Ours will be a foreign policy that keeps that ever in mind. Ours will be a foreign policy which recognizes that in international negotiations we must make no undue concessions; that in pursuing détente we must not grant unilateral favors with only the hope of getting future favors in return. Agreements that are negotiated, such as the one signed in Helsinki, must not take from those who do not have freedom the hope of one day gaining it. Finally, we are firmly committed to a foreign policy in which secret agreements, hidden from our people, will have no part. Honestly, openly, and with firm conviction, we shall go forward as a united people to forge a lasting peace in the world based upon our deep belief in the rights of man, the rule of law and guidance by the hand of God."

a highly explosive, gaseous cloud was suspended over the floor of the convention at that moment, and one spark would have blown the convention up. It was a very volatile situation. Then the "morality in government" plank came up. The press was playing it clearly as a slap at our administration and therefore it was, no matter what it actually said. So the problem was, how do you develop an argument against the plank if what you're arguing against is the press interpretation of it rather than its content? It would have been nonsense to try to make such an argument on the floor of the convention that night, after the vote on 16C. When it had become clear that we were winning 16C, I was in telephone communication with the president back at the hotel. I asked the vice president and others to come up from the convention floor because we had to make a decision and get guidance from the president. We had a meeting with about eight people, including the vice president, and agreed on the strategy of not challenging the plank. And then I suggested to the vice president that he call Secretary Kissinger.

NAUGHTON: Weren't there, in fact, some very private conversations between the Reagan and Ford people about what shape the foreign policy platform should take?

DUVAL: About a month before the convention, or maybe six weeks, there was a series of meetings.

BRODER: What turned out to be the crucial decision in the convention? What finally tipped it and sealed Reagan's defeat?

KEENE: It was probably the decision of Mississippi to go by unit rule against 16C, which scared the other votes that we [Reagan people] might have had in other delegations. But it could have been other things. I think that the procedural approach that we took was the correct approach. We could have won it if a very few people in the Mississippi delegation had decided to vote differently.

NOFZIGER: Reagan went in there behind, so it wasn't a question of how to keep from losing it but of how to win it. After looking at all the options, we went with 16C. There were a couple of other serious possibilities too, but I'm not sure that they would have made any difference.

KEENE: During the period leading up to the convention and during the convention itself, we were all doing a lot of thinking and talking about different approaches we might take. It was our conclusion, right or wrong, that the procedural approach that we took gave us our best chance of winning. The device of 16C was John Sears' idea originally, but everyone had talked about it before it was decided to go ahead with it.

NOFZIGER: The [Reagan] staff sat down and worked it out and presented it to the governor in Kansas City. We went over the options and the pros and cons, and he put his seal of approval on it.

KEENE: In general, Governor Reagan delegated a lot of responsibility, but he did maintain for himself the right of ultimate review and the establishment of the tone of what he said. The governor had a great deal of faith in John Sears, and this allowed us to move quickly in making decisions. The Reagan campaign was under the direction of one person, and under ordinary circumstances, there wasn't very much disagreement among the staff; and Governor Reagan did not second guess his manager on questions of a practical nature.

The question really is whether there was a way to have won with the procedural approach. It was close enough so that I think if a few things had fallen the other way, we might have won it. The main task of the Ford campaign in the convention was to keep the wrong decisions from being made. We were hoping that the Ford people would make some mistakes that we could capitalize on, but they did not make very many mistakes in the convention and so there wasn't much there that we could capitalize on. They had the votes there and they had to hold on to them, and they were following good advice on how to do it.

FORD CONVENTION STRATEGY

TEETER: I was not involved in the convention or the convention management at all, but I know that we [Ford people] wanted to come out of the convention without the perception of having made any blunders—come out of it looking like a winner, with a good acceptance speech and approval of the vice presidential candidate. Jim Baker [Ford's chief delegate hunter] seemed to feel very confident, going into the convention and continuing all the way through, that the Ford people could control the situation on any level, without any consternation.

OTTEN: After that error-ridden primary campaign, what suddenly changed?

DUVAL: The Reagan challenge forced us to develop the capability to win. A lot of that capability depended on having a clearly defined decision process, the right people, and the toughness it takes to get rid of people who aren't performing. By the second week in August, the president had a clear strategy of how he was going to win the election, and that meant winning the nomination. The strategy was in writing, it was lengthy, it was documented, he had gone over it very carefully, and it became a baseline against which to judge every decision he had to make. In addition, some very good people came up, including Jim Baker, who was in charge of the delegate operation, and Bill Timmons and some of his key people, who took over our convention control operation.

We needed good discipline at the convention. For example, we arrived in Kansas City the week before the convention, as the platform hearings were starting. As we entered the hall where the platform organization meeting was scheduled, a couple of reporters ran up and said that [North Carolina Senator] Jesse Helms and a band of merry men had come and tried to take over the Republican platform committee. They had passed a resolution before we arrived saying that the committee chairmen and subcommittee chairmen designated by the Republican National Committee were out of the window. We had to decide whether to use our people and overturn that vote. If we went in there and overplayed it, we would be confirming exactly what many of the delegates committed to Governor Reagan, and some undecideds, already thought about us. So we came in the next morning and did not challenge the vote, but had a show of presence. It was clear that we had the votes—we had a great many people there, in radio communication, and everybody was lined up. We made no attempt to overturn the vote, but established a clear presence of very firm control. As a result of that, there was a new election and, with one exception, every person who had agreed to serve in a leadership position was elected. So that was an example of not overplaying our hand.

NOFZIGER: There was a conservative faction at the convention that had some very specific ideas on what the platform should contain, and our [Reagan] people had to sit down and work things out with them before the platform was actually put in final form. The candidates had previously reached pretty general agreement, though; so while there was some discussion with Jesse Helms and others, I don't think they wound up with the final say on any part of the platform.

SELECTION OF DOLE

SNIDER: At what point was [Kansas] Senator Dole selected [as Ford's running mate]? Was there any consideration given to Governor Reagan, and if so, was he actually approached?

TEETER: Discussions about the vice presidential selection began four or five weeks before the convention, and we discussed a number of criteria: first, that the nominee be someone qualified to become president; second, that it be someone who might help us on a national basis across the country in terms of political appeal; third, that it be someone who would be a good campaigner, since we didn't feel the president was going to campaign a great deal in the fall; fourth, that it be someone who would get nominated in the convention, which was not an overwhelmingly Ford-controlled convention, and who would help unify the party after the convention was over; and last, that it be someone who would get immediately favorable reaction from the public and the press. Two or three of us discussed fairly long lists of people with the president, and there was a very small amount of polling done on the subject. Then about two weeks before the convention, we had some discussions at Camp David that focused on a much smaller group of people. At this point, Dick Cheney [Ford's chief of staff], Bryce Harlow [Ford adviser], Stu Spencer [political consultant], and I were involved in the discussions. Leaving Camp David, I think that we had a long list of eight or nine people, and drawn from that group, a short list of four or five chief prospects.

The discussion then resumed during the convention in Kansas City, about twice a day during that time, and Vice President Rockefeller and Jack Marsh, counsellor to the president, joined the rest of us. On Wednesday night, after the president had been nominated, we met, along with Mel Laird [former secretary of defense], from about 1:30 until 5:30 in the morning; and somewhere in the middle of that session, we were also joined by Senator Griffin [of Michigan] and Senator Tower [of Texas]. This discussion focused largely on a relatively short list of people—about four or five. It was my feeling that there were two categories of people that the president had to think about. Governor Reagan and Governor Connally [of Texas] were people who had a much higher awareness in the polling data; you couldn't compare them on the basis of polls with the other people on the list. We wanted the president to think about them in one category, and then the other list of names. The discussion adjourned about 5:30 in the morning, and then we all came back at 8:30 or 9:00, at which time the president made his final selection and it was announced later that day. The names that were most seriously discussed, in addition to Senator Dole, were Senator Baker [of Tennessee], Bill Ruckelshaus [former deputy attorney general], and Anne Armstrong [ambassador to the U.K.].

NOFZIGER: When he talked to Governor Reagan on Wednesday night, the president mentioned three or four names, including Senator Dole, and the governor said that he thought Senator Dole would be an acceptable vice president as far as he was concerned.

NAUGHTON: There was an impression abroad on Wednesday night that Governor Reagan might be willing to accept a draft, either to prevent the nomination of someone more liberal than conservatives would have wanted, or to get himself on the ticket. Was that a live possibility?

NOFZIGER: There were a lot of people in the California delegation trying to start a draft Reagan movement, and the governor made it as clear as he could that he would not accept it.

OTTEN: Certainly the impression was also abroad that one of the reasons that Bill Ruckelshaus was ruled out was that either Governor Reagan himself or key Reagan people had objected to him.

TEETER: There were a lot of impressions abroad, but the reports we [Ford people] got on the meeting of President Ford and Governor Reagan were substantially different from what I heard from reporters talking about impressions abroad. There was a lot of inaccurate dreaming going on in the press that night.

BRODER: Are you saying that the reports you got from the president and direct contacts with senior staff did not convey any sense of a Reagan veto of any of the people Ford was considering?

TEETER: The report we got from the president on his meeting with Governor Reagan was that there was no discussion of the people we had talked about seriously.

PERRY: But the only thing we have heard here that points positively to the selection of Dole is the fact that Reagan said he was acceptable.

NOFZIGER: I think that the governor may have discussed also the drawbacks some of the other people might have. In discussing the pros and cons of a possible candidate, it doesn't necessarily have to come down to saying, "This man is not acceptable to me, Ronald Reagan." You can point out that a certain possible candidate might have some weaknesses within a part of the party, or something like that.

BRODER: What were the positive factors that finally argued for the choice of Dole?

TEETER: There seemed to be two or three. He was a very popular figure within the party. He had been national chairman, and most people thought he would be an effective campaigner because of the speaking and traveling he had done as national chairman. He was not seen as someone who would alienate any ideological wing—he clearly was a very popular senator among his colleagues, liberal, moderate, and conservative. I don't know of any senators who objected to him at all. Like many vice presidential selections, he really had the least negative points.

SIEGEL: I never will understand this vice presidential choice. The two most important criteria for a vice president would seem to be competence and the ability to lead the nation if necessary, and I'll never really believe that the president thought his person was the most qualified. But beyond that, it would seem in pragmatic terms that the ticket would have to in some way reach out beyond hard core Republicans to independents and leaning Democrats as well. The question I posit to the Ford people is, did Bob Dole fit that reach-out category in terms of drawing Democrats and independents into the Republican column? And to the Reagan people, in light of the governor's sensitivity to the coalition-building aspects of a ticket, as seen in his own attempt to build the ticket with Schweiker and broaden the base of the party, did he find that this Ford-Dole ticket met the criteria that he had established for his own vice presidential selection?

SNIDER: The fact is that all the evidence we had on the Democratic side indicated that only a combination of Reagan and Ford could beat the thirty-four point lead that had been amassed. All of our polls indicated that the only Republican who could draw the independents and the Democrats to that side was Governor Reagan.

KEENE: The problems Mr. Ford and Mr. Reagan faced at the convention were different. One of the reasons that Senator Schweiker made a lot of sense for the Reagan ticket was that we had a need to go out in that direction, to find somebody who would tie the liberal wing of the party back into the Reagan candidacy. Mr. Ford at that point in the convention already had that wing of the party, and most of his problems were on the other side. There is a tendency to use the vice presidency to try and solve problems within the party at the convention. It would be reasonable to look at the Dole selection as a defensive move on the president's part, because there were problems in some of the farm states, for instance. Governor Reagan and Mr. Ford did not have the same problems in selecting a vice presidential candidate—because they came at it from different directions within the party, the correct selection for one might not be the correct selection for the other.

NOFZIGER: Had President Ford picked a liberal Republican, I'm not certain that Governor Reagan would have been able to control the conservatives on the floor of the convention. I think that the president faced the possibility of a heavily split party even if he had been able to push a liberal Republican through. I suspect that the vote on, say, Ruckelshaus, might have been as close as the vote on Ford and Reagan themselves.

TEETER: I think you have to assume that Senator Dole met the president's criteria for a vice president, since the president made the decision to choose him. That's completely separate from the question of whether Reagan could have gotten Senator Schweiker through the convention, or whether the president could have gotten through someone who was not acceptable to the conservative delegates in the convention.

DEARDOURFF: It's interesting to think about whether the president could have won that fight on the floor. I don't consider that the Ford people made enough of the fact, which I believe to be true, that Bill Ruckelshaus had been the first person to whom John Sears had gone prior to the time he went to Schweiker. Ruckelshaus might have been made more acceptable if that word had been spread more widely. Also, I never have understood why it would have been bad to have that fight even if it meant a vote as close as or closer than 16C, because it would have signaled something very important to the 82 percent of the people in the country who were non-Republicans. If the party was split and lost the 8.5 or 9 percent who fall into the far right side, would it have lost the election? I doubt it. Although we were not involved in the campaign at that time and therefore did not have direct access to the president, my partner Doug Bailey and I wrote a long memorandum suggesting that the president should, if necessary, precipitate that fight on the floor of the convention in order to get the kind of vice presidential candidate necessary to win the general election—even if it meant a really hard, knock-down, drag-out fight at the convention. Then, if he had lost, the president had the option of saying, "I either have my choice or I don't run."

TEETER: There was divided opinion in our [Ford] group at the time as to whether or not a fight would be a good thing. I don't think it would necessarily have been a bad thing, unless the president couldn't get his choice nominated, or unless his choice precipitated a Reagan draft that Reagan could not control. Some well-known liberals within the Republican party met with the president the morning before the announcement, at 8:30 or 9:00, and told him that they thought there was a real danger of a Reagan draft at that point, and that there were a limited number of people whom he could get through the convention. Vice President Rockefeller agreed strongly that this was the case.

KEENE: It's important to recall the atmosphere at the convention at that point. The vote on 16C had been very close. There were a number of Reagan people who had voted against 16C on its merits; there were a number of other people—some of them Ford delegates— who had bought the line that if 16C were defeated, they might be able to get Reagan or Connally or someone like that for vice president. Many of the people who had voted against 16C were the leaders of an effort to try to get Reagan to accept a draft, and the governor met with them to stop that. If those people then had been presented with Bill Ruckelshaus or someone of that sort, I think there's a very real possibility that a situation would have developed that Governor Reagan could not have controlled. I think there would have been real danger of a blowup on the floor, and there were people at the convention who would have welcomed that. Governor Reagan was not one of them. We [Reagan people] had entered the race with the intention of running the hardest, cleanest fight that we could and coming out with a united party, whoever the nominee might be. If the decision had been made to push Bill Ruckelshaus or someone of that sort, we would not have come out with a united party. We might have come out with no party at all.

PAUL SIMON (chairman, Draft Humphrey Committee): Do you think Dole was the strongest candidate you could have emerged with and still have had a united convention?

NOFZIGER: Probably three or four people would have been equally strong, but I'm not sure that there was anybody stronger.

NAUGHTON: Why was Reagan not willing to go on the ticket himself, for the sake of the party and the president's prospects and the conservative point of view?

NOFZIGER: He used to say early on that only the lead dog gets a change of scenery. But beyond that, he felt he could campaign just as effectively for the party without being the vice presidential nominee. Also, he felt it would be very difficult for him to be vice president and thus be forced to support views that didn't coincide with his own, especially when in eight years he would be seventy-three years old. The vice presidency is a good spot to be in if you're looking forward to being president eight years hence; it is not particularly the most effective spot to be in if you want to propound your own political philosophy and have no future beyond the vice presidency.

SIEGEL: At the Democratic National Committee, we were delighted by the selection of Dole. We were afraid it would be Ruckelshaus, which would have capitalized on our potential weakness among Catholics, especially in the Northeast. When we heard it was Dole, we thought immediately that this would draw added attention to [Democratic vice presidential candidate] Fritz Mondale, and that the Dole-Mondale contrast would become very evident during the campain.

DECISIVE FACTORS

BRODER: Looking back on it now, what were the decisive factors that finally made Gerald Ford rather than Ronald Reagan the nominee of the Republican party?

WIRTHLIN: The loss in New Hampshire structured all that followed. We [Reagan people] played catch-up ball from that time on. Between the time of the last primary and the convention, I was looking ahead toward the possibility of a Reagan candidacy in the general election, and it was clear at that point that we were really fighting two battles: first, the struggle for delegates; and second, the public polls and our private work indicated that both Reagan and Ford were losing strength in the potential battle against Carter. According to a late June–early July survey that we did, there was indication that while Carter had about a 20 percent lead over both Reagan and Ford, his base was extremely fluid. Nevertheless, there were some disturbing signals. Our data indicated that for the first time Carter was developing a base among the middle class and that, quite to our surprise, those who were most anti-Washington in their attitudes were going for Carter and not for Reagan. On the other hand, we found great incongruence in what people felt Carter's stands were on about five or six different test issues and what they in fact were. Interestingly, among that group who correctly knew Carter's positions, the gap between Carter and Reagan was only 12 percent. Contrarily, among those who had misperceived or just didn't know Carter's positions on these same six test issues, the gap between Carter and Reagan was 30 percent.

Thus, in July we considered moving Reagan into a more active anti-Carter mode, rather than an anti-Ford position, challenging Carter directly on the issues. By emphasizing Reagan's own strengths as an articulate and effective campaigner, we might have taken some of the sting out of fighting an incumbent president. Using what we perceived to be a really serious Carter weakness, we could possibly have gained some additional strength for Reagan in the national polls and thus perhaps have encouraged some of the delegates who were sitting on the fence to lean our way. The decision was made not to do this, but rather to go after the Catholic ethnics, primarily because budget and time constraints crowded in on that decision. My feeling is that if we had taken on Carter rather dramatically at that juncture, we possibly could have brought in some delegates and surely have helped Reagan in the polls. It also would have prepared the way for whoever won the nomination.

BRODER: Was the Reagan-Ford fight basically decided by tactical considerations, or were there other factors that were fundamental?

NOFZIGER: You have a bunch of people on one side who are highly concerned about issues and principles, a bunch of people on the other side who are highly concerned, and then you always have in the middle the people that both sides can get at, and that's where tactics come in.

TEETER: In dealing with the people who were essentially the regular Republicans, the nonideological people, the tactical considerations were most important, though there was some ebb and flow of ideology and issues which moved them. As for the Ford-Reagan fight as a whole, New Hampshire certainly set the tone. If that had been different, the result might well have been different. The decision of the Reagan people not to go into Ohio, Pennsylvania, and New Jersey was also crucial. And finally, the incumbency and the ability to use the White House were of great importance—for instance, in persuading the delegates after the primaries were over.

MAHE: We ought to mention two major factors in the outcome of the New Hampshire race: first, the return of Stu Spencer to the Ford campaign in October—in my opinion, they would not have won New Hampshire without him; and second, the impact of Mr. Reagan's speech about $90 billion—Ford would not have won New Hampshire if Governor Reagan had not been on the defensive.

WIRTHLIN: In New Hampshire, taxes have historically been a sensitive, critical issue; and everywhere Governor Reagan went, he had to respond to questions about the $90 billion and what impact this might have for New Hampshire's taxes. So he was forced to respond to that issue rather than develop other issues that would have given him more political leverage. Prior to the kick off of the New Hampshire primary, we tried to develop a simple, clear statement that would allow us to stop burning up our resources on the $90 billion statement, but it just didn't wash. The press and the Ford people kept the governor very much on the defensive.

TUCHMAN: It seems that everybody is saying that issues in this campaign were just what the candidates talked about, just the vehicle for expressing leadership qualities or lack of leadership qualities.

KEENE: The fact that the Reagan challenge, particularly in the early primaries, was a leadership challenge doesn't mean that the issues weren't important. You can demonstrate leadership in a direction nobody wants to go, and that's not going to do you much good. The issues were important, and Ronald Reagan cared a great deal about them. First of all, leadership itself was an issue—whether one could give a sense of direction to the country at a time when a lot of people questioned whether the country had any direction. Second, Governor Reagan, like Jimmy Carter in the Democratic party, addressed himself to the very real concern of the American people that an ever-encroaching government is making more and more decisions that people would rather make themselves. Third, in the foreign policy area, there was very serious concern about the United States' role in detente.

TUCHMAN: But the first point you mentioned was personality; and on the second point, they were both on the same side.

MAHE: Between Ford and Reagan, I think there were issues of style but no issues of substance in terms of real difference.

DEARDOURFF: The fact that the president was the president was the crucial factor in how the race came out. If it had been Reagan against Ford and Ford had not been president, he would have lost.

NOFZIGER: The incumbency is definitely what made the difference. It made the difference in New Hampshire, and it made the difference wherever Ford won all the way down to and including the convention.

WATTENBERG: What made Ford the presidential nominee was, in my judgment, what almost made him the winner in the general election. The summer of 1976 was a remarkably placid moment in American life, unheard of for almost a decade. Everybody said there was going to be a riot in New York during the July 4 celebration, but there wasn't; there was that remarkable machine up on Mars; there was the Olympics; there was an unusually peaceful Democratic convention, and a very gentlemanly Republican convention, considering what everybody said. Particularly after years and years of turbulence, this placid atmosphere redounded enormously to the benefit of the incumbent president. If we were going through a period of enormous turbulence, that would have been terrible for the incumbency.

KEENE: The Reagan polls reflected the fact that there was a gradually increasing confidence in the president on the part of the people, and I think this was played masterfully in the November election, and correctly so, by the Ford campaign.

WIRTHLIN: But underneath the placid exterior, there were some very strong and turbulent emotions. Inflation, unemployment, the scars of Watergate, and the memories of Viet Nam were very much in the election choice mix of many Americans even if they were to some degree suppressed. In the closing days of the general election,

Watergate in particular began to resurface as a key vote determinant among that group that remained undecided almost down to election day.

ROBERT J. KEEFE (campaign director for Jackson): Did the media make much difference in the Republican nominating process? For example, in the New Hampshire primary, why was Governor Reagan allowed to look like he was made to look in the commercials that were aired for him there? That could easily have tipped it the wrong way.

KEENE: All the media experts told us and told Governor Reagan that he had to go with the spots that he was using—and he did. Governor Reagan would occasionally say, "You know, when I ran in California, I just went on television and talked to the people, and they voted for me, so maybe we ought to do that." And all the experts said, "You can't go on television for half an hour and talk to people—they'll all go to sleep, change channels, or get upset because you preempted S.W.A.T.—you've got to go with these spots." We finally got into the use of that half hour in North Carolina. A lot of people were saying, "It's over, we're losing, we can't afford to take polls anymore, we can't afford to do anything, so let's at least let Governor Reagan talk to the people." But the very existence of that program was almost accidental. In the latter days of the Florida campaign, many of the stations would offer free time so they wouldn't have to sell it to you. When one of the network affiliates in Miami offered us a half hour, we discovered that our candidate didn't have a half hour television tape to put on the air because we had been listening to all the experts. So we arranged for him to sit down at a desk, with no set to speak of, and talk into the camera for a half hour—which he did—so they'd have a free tape to use in Miami. We kept a copy of the tape and when we got to North Carolina, and everything else seemed to have failed, we gave out that half hour tape. The *New York Times*, among other papers, gave that television tape a great deal of credit for the outcome of the North Carolina primary. From that point on, everyone agreed that Ronald Reagan was right and all the experts were wrong, so we started doing it his way, which we should have done in the first place.

WIRTHLIN: In preparing the early spots, the media people seemed to be overly concerned about making Ronald Reagan look too slick— too much like an actor. Right from the beginning our surveys indicated that was not a problem. There were only about 3 percent who even mentioned he was an actor, and those 3 percent mentioned it in a positive context.

KEENE: One of the things that made the race so close at the end was that everything made a difference. When you look at it with hindsight, it is very easy to say, "Well, we shouldn't have spent so much time in California, we should have spent it in Ohio. We should have run in New Jersey, we should have done this, we should have done the other thing." Looking at it in retrospect, those are obviously things we [Reagan people] should have done; but at the time it wasn't that clear.

Still, some things clearly did make a difference: one was the value of the incumbency, and another was the early momentum that the president had as a result of his victory in New Hampshire. Decisions that involved money were crucial too. We have talked about the decisions not to go into states like New York or New Jersey in a big way because of financial considerations in part. Equally important was the fact that because of the cash crunch and because of the unavailability of money, we wrote off states that we should have done better in. We wrote off the Maryland primary [May 18], though we finally spent a few dollars there in the last few days when all we could do was shotgun it out in the media where it didn't do us any good. We wrote off West Virginia [May 11]—we spent hardly any money there. We spent very little money in a lot of states at times when it could have been crucial. We had to write off Wisconsin [April 6] and leave because we probably wouldn't have had any place to sleep if we had stayed, and they might even have taken our airplane away from us and that could have been embarrassing. At that point, we didn't have any polls in Wisconsin, and we couldn't afford to take any. If we had had some money, if our candidate had been able to campaign there, we might have done much better than we did. I know that this is true of other campaigns too; but if I had to choose the most important factor in the Reagan campaign, I'd have to say it was finances.

TEETER: Finances were a problem for the Ford campaign as well. During the months of May and June and afterwards, there were a number of decisions that were made on financial grounds—places where the president went or didn't go, how much time he spent, and the amount of advertising that went into the individual states. Organizational money was essentially zero from about mid-May on. Not only did we have to worry about getting delegates in a contested situation, but we had to keep the headquarters open and in full operation for six weeks longer than the Democrats did, just simply because of the timing of the convention . So we were using that much more of the $10 million. There were times around the first of July when we thought the president and all of us might go to Kansas City on a Greyhound.

KEENE: All in all, I think that both the Reagan and Ford sides pulled punches at some points in the nomination process. Both sides could have been tougher, and they might have got some advantage out of it. But the instructive lesson for Republicans, at least, in 1976 was that you could have a contest, you could have a totally contested convention with some strong feeling, and still come out with a united party. Some disagreed with the outcome of the convention, and none of us like the way the election turned out; but the fact is that the Ford people and the Reagan people, because of the handling of the campaign on both sides, were able to get together and run a pretty effective campaign in the general election.

❋ *Chapter 2*

The Democratic Nomination

Groundwork. Mondale Withdrawal. Early Starters. "Brokered" Convention? Iowa Caucus. Mood of the Country. Strategies for Early Primaries. Black Vote. Subsequent Strategies. "Fuzziness" Issue. Potential Humphrey Campaign. Late Primaries. Final Challengers. Carter for Sure. Selection of Mondale. Role of Labor, Blacks, and Party Leaders.

JAMES M. PERRY (columnist, *National Observer*): As we begin a discussion of the Democratic primaries, I'd like to mention a couple of dates to establish a context. In September 1974 Edward Kennedy withdrew from the nomination race for personal considerations; in December 1974 a Gallup poll asked voters to select their first choice for the nomination from a list of thirty-one names, including George Wallace, Hubert Humphrey, Henry Jackson, George McGovern, John Lindsay, Adlai Stevenson, Ralph Nader, Walter Mondale, on through Terry Sanford and Kevin White—but not including Jimmy Carter.

GROUNDWORK

MARK A. SIEGEL (executive director, Democratic National Committee): A still earlier date to mention is December 9, 1972, when Bob Strauss was elected chairman of the Democratic National Committee in what was perceived to be a factional victory. From December 1972 through March 1973, Strauss and his staff attempted to rebuild a working coalition in the party. In March 1973, at the first meeting of the committee after the Strauss election, items that didn't seem terribly important were decided—the selection of at large members of the committee, the selection of additional members of the charter commission and delegate selection commissions—but these decisions were important in terms of the goal and the process. From December 1972 through the committee convention in December 1974, our job was to review the rules of the party and to change them in a meaningful way, but also to keep in mind that the process of that change was in itself crucial. We worked to develop the relationships among the "new politics" people and the party regulars, among elected officials and groups like black activists, feminists, and so forth, to get them to work together on building the groundwork for a successful primary period, convention, and general election. In 1973 we lived from delegate selection meeting to delegate selection meeting, and the coalition that we were trying to put together could have fallen apart at any point. We finally adopted new delegate selection rules that I think were improvements on the past.

In 1974 our main focus, aside from the elections which were coming up, was the 1974 midterm convention. Many people, especially people in the press, thought that the convention was a make-or-break kind of situation, where the Democratic party might very well destroy itself over structural policy and coalitions, where constituency groups that would be competing against each other in 1975 and 1976 for the nomination would be testing one another's strength. Things had exploded in August 1974 at Kansas City at the last meeting of the charter commission, when most blacks and some members of the party's reform movement walked out; but in December 1974 the midterm convention took place successfully, and we developed the first party charter in the history of either major political party. Everything could have broken apart at many points during 1972 to 1974. We had a long-range goal, of course, but we always concentrated on just keeping it together for the next month, and the next month.

MONDALE WITHDRAWAL

PERRY: On November 21, 1974, Fritz Mondale withdrew from the nomination race and said that he lacked the overwhelming desire to be president that is essential for the kind of campaigning required. Later on, it became more and more clear to everyone how difficult it was to run in thirty primaries over a long period of time.

RICHARD MOE (campaign director for Mondale): Senator Mondale started an exploratory effort about mid-1973, and continued it until November 1974, when he finally withdrew. Most of the effort was simply his traveling around the country. Contrary to the impression that was abroad then, he had not really decided to run, but was thinking seriously about it. He traveled about 200,000 miles, went into thirty states, met with all kinds of party and labor leaders, and did most of the things candidates do at that stage of the process. By the summer of 1974, he was campaigning five or six days a week for congressional candidates, and was concluding that he did not much like this way of life. He started debating with himself and some of his staff as to whether or not he really wanted to continue this life for two years, realizing that his chances at best were remote at that point. He liked to joke about how in the polls he was still three points behind Don't Know, and when he challenged Don't Know to a debate, he never got an answer. All candidates are frustrated in that early stage, because there's no tangible evidence of how well they're doing. In any case, by November 1974 it was clear that Senator Mondale had to decide whether he was going to go all out as a presidential candidate. If he did, it would involve asking a lot of people to make full-time commitments to him and to his efforts; it would mean substantial fundraising commitments; but most importantly in his mind, it would mean virtually abandoning the Senate. This last point weighed very heavily on him, and was, I think, the decisive factor that decided him against running—he loved the Senate, and he had seen other senators go to be candidates and never return to the Senate in quite the same way.

JAMES A. JOHNSON (deputy campaign manager for Mondale): What Senator Mondale was doing in 1974 was trying to discover what it would be like if he ran for president, and he came very close on a couple of occasions to saying that he was a candidate. He gave a 99 percent statement to a labor convention at one point, and there was a great deal of activity after Kennedy's withdrawal in the fall of 1974 and a very encouraging development of support. It was his view of his lifestyle, his political career, and his relationship to Minnesota that ultimately led him to decide that he didn't want to be a candidate; but there were many times during that period when he was testing the possibility. That was a period when everybody was wondering where the American electorate was, and it wasn't clear what kind of appeal was going to be well received. Senator Mondale finally made his decision, and he still feels confident that it was the decision he should have made.

EARLY STARTERS

PERRY: I'd like to hear about the other contenders—what their very early strategies were, what they hoped to accomplish. To start: I think it was no coincidence that Mondale's announcement was on November 21 and Udall entered two days later on November 23.

JOHN B. GABUSI (campaign director for Udall): Congressman Udall began in 1973, and spent 1974 much like Senator Mondale, though not at the same intensity. By the end of 1974, with two candidates gone from the left, we believed that we were in a good position. The Mondale announcement was the real key to the congressman's decision that he would in fact be a candidate, though he had been thinking about it for twelve months and had been moving around the country. We were in the same quandary that everybody else was: we didn't know who our constituency was at that point, and the climate of the country was negative and alienated. But we had some national constituencies that we assumed would be there— for example, the environmental movement—and our main hope in 1975 was to broaden his base through the normal activities of traveling, to develop a core staff, and to build a financial capability through direct mail in order to be prepared for the primaries.

ROBERT J. KEEFE (campaign director for Jackson): I joined the Jackson campaign on December 1, 1974, and had a million dollars in the bank, which was not an unhappy situation. Scoop had been moving around just like everybody else for a year or a year and a half; actually, I think he did not stop his 1972 campaign for the presidency, just continued it. In December 1974 we thought that our money problems would consist of running up against the spending limitations; we planned to raise $6 to $8 million in 1975. We thought that we were off to a good start and that we could just build on what Scoop had been doing for the past four years—carve out a niche in the middle of our party and let the other guys run around and kill themselves off on the left.

JAMES M. FRIEDMAN (campaign manager for Bayh): I joined the Bayh campaign relatively late in the game, about December 1, 1975. Instead of having a million dollars in the bank, I think we had some thousands. Of the major announced candidates who were around in 1975, Senator Bayh was the only one who had a major reelection effort on his hands in 1974. He won reelection in Indiana by about 1.5 percent of the vote, and that effort took all of his time and energy and financial resources. Consequently, while the presidential campaign and his own interests in it were certainly on his mind at that time, he had no opportunity to pursue the kinds of strategies that some of the other candidates were pursuing. After his November

1974 reelection, he decided to wait and see whether or not Congress-- man Udall or someone else on the left or center, having started earlier, would develop a viable candidacy. After thinking about it through the latter part of the spring of 1975, he decided during the summer to enter the primaries.

Other than Senator Church and Governor Brown, Senator Bayh was probably the latest to decide to run in the primaries, and that was the greatest handicap we had to face. It made it difficult organizationally, first of all, in terms of his ability to establish constituency contacts in the states he had targeted and to make the decisions to go into particular early caucuses and primaries, and also in terms of his ability to raise the money to fund the effort. Secondly, the late decision forced him into a relatively crowded part of the spectrum at that time, competing with four or five other declared candidates for approximately 40 or 50 percent of the Democratic constituency. In 1975 his strategy was a very simple one, and a relatively brutal one: he had to eliminate rather directly the other candidates clustered around us, right and left, particularly Congressman Udall. For that reason, the Bayh campaign targeted certain objectives in terms of caucuses, particularly the NDC [New Democratic Coalition] convention in New York [in December 1975], which assumed a symbolic importance out of all proportion to its real importance.

PERRY: What was Bayh's role in the development of this strategy?

FRIEDMAN: Senator Bayh played a very active role in ultimate approval of the campaign plan of action provided by the campaign manager, and also at the beginning in laying out what he wanted to do. Sometimes a candidate will make an initial suggestion and the staff will come back with comments and countersuggestions; the ultimate decision and direction will come out of such interaction. There is not a relationship of equality between the candidate and the top people in the campaign, but the candidate needs the strong input of his staff. If a candidate doesn't realize that he cannot judge everything that's going on and that he must accept the input of his staff, he is doomed to lose at every turn.

CHARLES S. SNIDER (campaign director for Wallace): During this early period, we were supposedly the old veterans of national politics, having run three times before. The Wallace campaign organization had actually got to the point where it was almost a business. From past experience we knew that the first thing we had to have was finances, so we were spending almost all of our time putting together what we needed to finance a campaign. Knowing that the election law was coming in, we started out to do as much prospecting as possible so that what we spent early on to put together and produce our prospects list would not be counted as part of our limited expenditures of $10 million. We got criticized for this, and people said that we spent $2 or $3 million more than anybody else. All the polls were showing us leading at that time, mainly because of name recognition. A major concern we had was not to make the same slip up that we did in 1972, when we didn't file the candidate's delegates properly. All in all, about 90 percent of our effort was spent on putting together a mailing list that would produce names for the campaign, and building the necessary organization to file delegates. We were successful in doing both of these things, but it turned out that the vote-getting ability of our candidate was not what it had been in the past. As a matter of fact, it almost seemed that the more we campaigned, the less our popularity was. Of course, at that point, we weren't too much concerned about Governor Carter, especially since he hadn't shown up in the polls at all.

JOSEPH L. POWELL, JR. (press secretary for Carter): On September 23, 1974, Senator Kennedy withdrew, and that signaled a major shift for us. We had thought that if we started early, without a reelection campaign to worry about or any duties of office to worry about, we could do very well against Senator Kennedy in New Hampshire, and then come down to Florida and take on Governor Wallace, and that was about as far as our planning went. After Florida, we would be either on the way or in trouble. We had assumed also that with Senator Kennedy in the race, there would probably be very few others running, that he would probably keep out the Udalls and the Mondales and the Bayhs. As soon as Kennedy got out, it became obvious that things were going to be a good deal more complex. As it turned out, though, we basically ended up the same way, even though we were running against a group in New Hampshire rather than a single candidate.

Looking at the whole early period, I think we were right in deciding not to worry during 1974 and 1975 about what things looked like from a national perspective, not to be too concerned that we weren't moving in the polls and that nobody was paying much attention. In fact, I think it was an asset for us that we didn't have people looking over our shoulders. In 1975 the level of expectations for Jimmy Carter was extremely low. Deciding not to worry about any of the things we couldn't do anything about gave us a certain amount of freedom to concentrate on the things that we could do something about—like beginning to establish organizations, almost on a person-to-person basis, in some of those early states.

PAUL SIMON (chairman, Draft Humphrey Committee): Following the Kennedy withdrawal, almost every poll showed that Humphrey had more support than all the other candidates combined. One night in early October 1975, seven of us—five Democrats and two Republicans—were sitting around during a lull in the House and talking about whom the two parties might nominate. I said, "If you were just to name the person who would be the best president of the United States, whom would you name?" We all seven named Hubert Humphrey. A month later, I was on a plane with Senator Humphrey and told him about this conversation and about what should be done, saying that the nomination ought not to go to someone just because he was ahead in the polls. Senator Humphrey said, "I think you're right, but I'm not going to do anything. The party knows where I stand. If they want me, I'm available, but I'm not going to lift a finger." So some of us in the House got together and decided we'd better check out the legal end of things. We found out that the federal election law just didn't contemplate a draft movement. I called Neil Staebler and Tom Curtis [members of the Federal Election Commission] and had some long conversations, particularly with Neil Staebler. I finally wrote a letter to the Federal Election Commission and asked what the financial status of a draft movement would be. There was a tentative decision that we could spend either $1,000 or $5,000 dollars, and if that were the case, we were dead. This was prior to the Supreme Court decision [in January 1976 interpreting the 1974 federal election law].

PETER P. CURTIN (political director for Church): Senator Church was one of the last to enter the campaign. We were expecting that no front runner would emerge, at least in the early part of the season. We were not expecting Governor Brown to enter the race at any point.

MICHAEL KANTOR (adviser to Shriver; campaign manager for Brown): In the summer of 1975 I was involved in some discussions with Sargent Shriver, having worked with him in his 1972 vice presidential efforts. Basically, the Shriver campaign had a conflict about where its constituency lay: was he the inheritor of the so-called Kennedy constituency (which I don't think exists except for Teddy Kennedy), or was he going to create for himself a constituency of his own, which I thought he had to do in order to be a legitimate candidate. As I saw it, that conflict was never resolved effectively. The campaign never positioned itself, nor understood where it was supposed to be, and therefore it never really got off the ground except in the summer of 1975. Interestingly enough, in terms of name recognition, in terms of potential, in terms of positive-negative ratio, Shriver was in pretty good shape, especially in New England; but there was never a coalescence of that constituency, never an understanding of what the problems were and what the opportunities were. Of course, the results showed this in Massachusetts, Vermont, and New Hampshire, and that was the end of the Shriver candidacy.

"BROKERED" CONVENTION?

FRIEDMAN: In November 1975, at the beginning of the active campaign for the early primaries, how many campaigns were affected in their strategic decisions by the belief that there was going to be a "brokered" convention—or to use a better term, a fragmented convention, with no one having a dominant position at the start? It seemed clear to me that a dominant figure would emerge from the long and complicated series of primaries; but I think the opposite belief influenced people to go into this state rather than that state, or to stay out of some states, and to count on negotiations with leadership.

JOHN M. QUINN (campaign director for Udall): We did not believe there would be a brokered convention. Our basic idea was that a win in either New Hampshire or Massachusetts and either Wisconsin or New York would lend further viability to the Udall campaign. Of course, if that didn't happen, and if no other candidate were to emerge with a very clear lead, then there might be a coalition-building process that would last longer than mid-April and might go down to the days of the convention.

JESSICA TUCHMAN (director of issues and research for Udall): Congressman Udall talked about this all the time. In his first campaign interview, with a *Congressional Quarterly* reporter, Mo kept saying it was going to be a brokered convention, and that was his way of saying, "Though I'm totally unknown now, there is going to be a brokered convention and that's why this campaign is a long shot but not impossible."

GABUSI: Congressman Udall could make the intellectual argument that there was a possibility of a brokered convention, but we could not operate a primary strategy on the assumption that we were going to end up with a brokered convention.

POWELL: The Carter campaign did not believe that there was going to be a brokered convention, and we operated on that assumption. It seemed to us that the whole idea of a brokered convention was just not consistent with American politics; it seemed to us to ignore the strongest sort of currents on the political scene. We thought that a large group of candidates would stay about even until the day they started counting votes, and then candidates would begin to fall out very rapidly. If we won a few at the beginning, it would give us a tremendous boost.

SIEGEL: I think much of the talk about a brokered convention was a product of the new rules. We [Democrats] were operating under proportional representation in a significant way for the first time in a multicandidate field; and a lot of people thought that because of proportional representation, the "winnowing-out" process would not occur.* The theory was that if several people could get 20 percent or 15 percent, no one at any point would get a majority; at no point would it be a one-on-one confrontation because everybody would stay in with his delegates so he could be a broker and force the convention. That was the theory that the press talked about so much.

KEEFE: The Jackson campaign did not think it would be a brokered convention. We thought that the process would have three stages: the early stage would narrow the field to about three people, and George Wallace would not be knocked out during that period; then there would be a Wallace challenge period in Northern states where he had done very well before, and some other candidate was going to have to beat George Wallace decisively in the North during that period; then there would be the run-offs between the couple of guys who were left.

BEN J. WATTENBERG (adviser to Jackson): During 1973 and particularly 1974, Scoop Jackson was getting more substantive publicity than the whole rest of the Senate put together—in terms of the energy crisis, the oil company question, the Russian emigrations, and the Kissinger fights—and not on the basis of running, but on the basis

---

*By the new rules of the Democratic party (with some important exceptions), a state's convention delegates reflect proportionately the votes cast for the various candidates in the state's primary.

of what he was doing, he had gone up to 13 or 14 percent in the Gallup polls. He had never been higher than 5 or 6 percent when he ran in 1972, and we were very encouraged by this development.

KEEFE: During 1973 and 1974, Scoop was doing extremely well, and the Senate base was providing him with a lot of very excellent press. Unfortunately, this all diminished in 1975 when the campaign got going and he stayed in the Senate. This caused us great concern in late August and September, so we thought we should do something dramatic in the presidential campaign to try to pull ourselves up and really become a front runner and a force to deal with. So in September we tried what John Sears tried very much later—we made an offer to another U.S. senator to be vice presidential candidate on Jackson's ticket. Muskie did not accept it, obviously. We thought he would be substantially beneficial for our campaign.

IOWA CAUCUS

PERRY: On to the results of the strategies. On January 19, 1976, the Iowa caucus was held, in which 10 percent of the state's registered Democrats took part. Carter got about 28 percent, Bayh came in second with 13 percent. Moving to New Hampshire on February 24, again Carter won with 29 percent and Udall came close with 24 percent, which surprised a lot of people.

POWELL: It seemed to be one of the lessons of the 1972 campaign that the early states get a lot of attention because they are the first things off the bat. This became even more crucial this year once Senator Kennedy was out, and there was a big field, and everybody, with a few exceptions like George Wallace and Senator Jackson, was bobbing around down there from asterisk to 3 percent. Everybody was looking for some reason to say, "Somebody's doing better than somebody else."

Iowa was a state where we [Carter people] profited in the beginning from unnaturally low expectations. If you look at the state—who the people are, what they do, what they think—it's not a bad state at all for a candidate like Jimmy Carter, but I think the perception was at the beginning that it would be absolutely foolish for him to go in. In fact, we were told by the state party chairman that we had a nice guy, but that it wasn't his kind of place and he shouldn't go in there. We finally scrambled around and got an invitation. The first trip in was to speak to a testimonial dinner for the oldest and longest-serving Democratic elected official in the state of Iowa, a lady named Marie Jahn, who was a court reporter. It was very successful—we had a couple of hundred people there who had come to see Miss Jahn, and whoever this other guy was. It went downhill from there. We moved into Sioux City and had a breakfast for fourteen; and then we had a reception where the only people who showed up were the two people from another town who were supposedly putting the thing on for us, and a couple of drop-ins. The state party chairman was so embarrassed at what had happened that he delegated someone to come over and get the governor to go shake hands around the courthouse. And this was the beginning of the Iowa thing in early 1975. The best thing we did was to put Tim Kraft in there, and he really went to work. There were some good people that really worked like hell when we weren't there, and I don't think we were there but twice in the first six months of 1975. We got two things out of Iowa—the final win, obviously, and the poll in late October [1975] that we won. More happened faster following that poll in Iowa than we had ever expected.

FRIEDMAN: Congressman Udall and Jimmy Carter had early visits in Iowa and had begun to think about it before Birch Bayh had even decided to run. Once he did decide to run, there was still not a significant consideration for Iowa. Bayh's first visit to Iowa took place in late October 1975, when there began to be a perception that because it was first, he should make a strong showing there. This would be a first step in our overall strategy of trying to eliminate Udall and Harris and Shriver. We [Bayh people] did not have anyone on the ground there until early December, when Dick Sykes came in from Indiana and did a good job for us in terms of reaching out to the constituency we were seeking. This was primarily a labor-based constituency, although our late start denied us a critical portion of it, particularly the auto workers, which was a serious loss. Unfortunately, everyone decided that we were doing very well, and that Senator Bayh had a chance to finish first. We would have been quite happy to do exactly as we did, which was to finish ahead of Udall, Shriver, and Harris, so as to establish our credibility. We didn't take seriously enough the damage that could be done to us by allowing other people to set a high expectation for our performance in Iowa. Our budget allocation for Iowa was probably the least of any of the candidates. Just a week or two prior to the caucus, most of the other candidates went to mass media, radio, newspaper, and some TV, and we did none of that, but did a little bit of mailing to former caucus attendees. We were happy to finish second, but it was perceived by other people that we hadn't done as well as we were supposed to.

POWELL: Senator Bayh actually did a hell of a job, coming in late, and got burned on expectations. We [Carter people] thought the thing was a lot closer than it turned out to be. So our contribution to raising expectations for Bayh was entirely sincere. The day before the caucus, Hamilton Jordan and I were up there calling precinct lists —that's how much we believed it.

TUCHMAN: The press was talking all the time about whether New Hampshire was going to be allowed again to be the whole ballgame again, or whether Iowa's coming first would change that this time. In the Udall campaign, I don't think we ever got it straight in our heads. We didn't think that New Hampshire was going to be absolutely crucial, but we didn't decide until too late whether Iowa was going to be important or not. The other thing that dominated our thinking in 1975 was the necessity of getting a base built in twenty states. It was so easy to get the first twelve that people forgot about the last eight. For us, the problem of time was also a terrible one all the way through 1975, because Congressman Udall felt he had to be in the Congress four days a week—that was a constant struggle for us.

JOHNSON: Senator Mondale and his group very early identified Iowa as a place where he would have to do well, and he spent a lot of time in districts there during the 1974 election. At that time there seemed to be a great deal of interest in Udall. In fact, Udall was probably the figure most mentioned by the people we were talking to as someone who was likely to do well in the Iowa caucus. It was never clear to me what happened in 1975 through early January 1976 in terms of Udall's performance.

QUINN: By late November and early December and January, we [Udall people] were fighting Bayh in a very defensive manner. We felt that the "winnowing-out" process should not take place either too early—at the NDC convention [in December] or the Iowa caucus [in January]—or too late—in New York [April 6], where Bayh was financially and organizationally very much together. We went into Iowa realizing that we were going to get a black eye, hoping to elevate people's expectations of Bayh and also not allow him to break out of that liberal pack at that early point. Although it did not get a lot of media attention, the fact was that there were a lot of uncommitted delegates in Iowa, most of whom we felt were for Humphrey. While Carter was getting the media attention, we felt encouraged by the Humphrey support. We felt things would start to move our way in New Hampshire and Massachusetts [March 2], if ever.

GERALD RAFSHOON (media director for Carter): The Carter campaign tried to foster a lot of excitement in the Iowa caucus. Knowing the domino effect of what a win in Iowa would do to our chances in New Hampshire and then Florida [March 9], we decided we had to win. We went on television to get new people to come into the caucus. We didn't do a mailing to the traditional Democratic list; when we decided to go on television, we mailed schedules to every old caucus attendee but also tried to excite people to come to the caucus who had never been before.

MOOD OF THE COUNTRY

PATRICK H. CADDELL (pollster for Carter): From 1974, our surveys were finding a growing sense of pessimism in people, not only about the country but also about their own lives. People were suspicious about the political process, had rising doubts about its efficacy. Something like 68 percent of the people believed that their leaders in the last decade had consistently lied to them, for instance; and there was also a sense that the government mostly didn't work, but when it did, it seemed to work against people. There was a reaction against the government and Congress and Washington, and a search for new leadership, without any idea of where that leadership was coming from. Watergate had helped to create almost a nonideological approach on the part of a lot of people. On one level, there was a desire for change, for a lot of reform in the country, but not defined in an ideological way; there was also a yearning for the restoration of basic values. This was almost a contradictory impulse—combining pessimism and hopefulness—and it was evident throughout the primaries and into the general election.

In the early stages of the campaign, the only candidate that had any real recognition at all was George Wallace. By 1975 he had become a symbol of a lot of frustration, and he scored higher in the polls than he ever did in 1972. Yet it was clear that a lot of his support was amorphous. When we first looked at this support in Florida, we could tell that there really were two constituencies: a hard core Wallace support, which was much smaller than the hard core Wallace support in 1972; and then the people attracted to him as a symbol of their frustration. The other candidates were all relatively unknown, and it was a very open situation. What I think Carter identified early in his own travels was some sense of people's yearning for change and restoration.

PETER D. HART (pollster for Udall): While we're on the subject of general conditions during the early campaign period, I'd like to cite a survey we did of the 2,000 delegates to the Democratic forum held in Louisville in November 1975. The one thing that struck me in that poll was the indication of a tremendous desire to win on the part of all the various Democratic factions. This was important in the general election and the way in which the Democratic party came together, and it was something we saw very early. In the months of November, December, and early January, we did seven surveys in Missouri, Illinois, California, New Jersey, Tennessee, Indiana, and Iowa. We asked a series of questions related to the mood of the country—how people felt about the issues, what they thought about the presidential candidates—and most of the things we found were similar to what Pat Caddell found. When we asked them if they felt the country was generally going in the right direction or was seriously off on the wrong track, we found that, by a margin of about three to one, they said things were seriously off on the wrong track. Obviously, this was working very much against the Republicans. At the same time, we were finding that Ford was in deep trouble, that his job rating was about 32–68, 35–65, depending on the state. In every state, Tennessee or California or Iowa or whatever, it was always heavily negative; you could differentiate the rating more in terms of age groups or things like that than you could by regions of the country. We also found a very depressed spirit—people were very much down on the way things were going in general and especially in the economy.

One other thing, which relates more to the general election: we gave people a list of about twenty different adjectives, and asked them to pick two or three qualities that they'd like the next president of the United States to have. They were very action-oriented. They were obviously looking for integrity and trustworthiness, but they were looking particularly for leadership and the ability to get things done. When we asked them to choose the adjectives that described Ford, they saw him as a good family man, patriotic, and honest. So there was a difference between what they wanted and what they were getting. As we measured the Democratic primary candidates during this period, we found that between 30 and 40 percent of the voters had no choice. We were asking them, from a list of nine candidates, who their first choice was, who their second choice was, and who was unacceptable to them no matter what happened. It depended on the state, but sometimes either Wallace or Jackson was in the lead. In some of our early states, Jackson would be in the lead with maybe 15 or 16 percent and Wallace with maybe 13 percent. When we looked at the unacceptable quotient, we found both Shriver and Wallace to be through because both of them had a high percentage of unacceptability. It was simply a totally fluid situation where nobody had caught on. It was wide open in all the states.

STRATEGIES FOR EARLY PRIMARIES

PERRY: Given all this that we know, what were the primary strategies of the candidates, and what impact did they have?

POWELL: After Iowa, the goal of the Carter campaign was to win in New Hampshire—we almost had to. We certainly profited from the enthusiasm after Iowa, and I think we were successful in creating the one candidate opposition—us against everybody else—by painting Congressman Udall and Senator Bayh as being all of one piece.

RAFSHOON: We made New Hampshire a showcase for presenting Jimmy Carter—as the candidate from outside of Washington, as the centrist, as the Democratic candidate who could win the election. It was very important for us to win the first major Northern primary. And a win in New Hampshire would mean that we would be taken more seriously in Florida, where we were closing in on Wallace. A lot of our time and all the money we had were being spent in New Hampshire. We understood the media, and so we knew that our candidate would get a lot of attention in New Hampshire because the press was giving so much attention there.

PERRY: Did Governor Carter himself participate in working out this strategy?

RAFSHOON: The governor always knew the concepts we were operating from, and we talked to him about our strategy from time to time; but our decisionmaking about New Hampshire was prompted by what we were reading in the press, and what was happening in Iowa. We didn't have very many meetings. Jody [Powell] was with Jimmy on the road, Hamilton [Jordan] was in one place and I was in another, and Mr. Kirbo [Carter adviser] was downtown. We each realized that whatever we read the night before, we would see on television the next night; and so I felt that I had to increase the media, and Hamilton felt he had to book a few more days of the governor's time in New Hampshire, and Bob Lipshutz [Carter's campaign treasurer] felt he would have to find the money for creditors. It just fell into place.

POWELL: There weren't a lot of decisions to make at that point. There weren't many ways to win it. Once we [Carter people] decided how we were going to go about it, there wasn't much point in trying to refigure the damn thing, because there was only one road open and either it was going to work out or it wasn't. The relationship of New Hampshire to Florida and the South generally is important. One of the major things that we had going for us against Governor Wallace in Florida was that Jimmy Carter was a Southerner also, and we could profit from that by convincing people that Carter was a Southerner with a real chance to win the nomination. Obviously, there's no better way to do that than to go 'way the hell off yonder to New Hampshire and win a primary. Our win in New Hampshire had a greater impact, I think, on Southern voters than it did in the rest of the country. The New Hampshire primary seemed very important, particularly to people who think about politics as most people do—about every fourth month for fifteen minutes—and for a Southerner to go up there and win that primary was tremendously significant.

RAFSHOON: Florida was the big one for us. Our [Carter's] theme in Florida was, "Now we can stop sending messages and send the President," and winning New Hampshire validated that theme.

KEEFE: You were using the North in the South and the South in the North. In your fundraising appeals in the North, you were suggesting that you could take care of Mr. Wallace once and for all in the South and so help us up here.

WATTENBERG: In my judgment, Jackson's decision not to go into New Hampshire was probably the critical thing for the Carter campaign, because it allowed Carter to be described by the national media as the only nonliberal in the state while they grouped everybody else together. The senator made this decision himself—he made the same decision in 1972 and 1976, and I think he made the wrong decision.

KEEFE: Henry Jackson was not a new quantity in American politics, and he had a very strong image of being a loser—a guy you couldn't take seriously because he was not going anyplace. Probably the worst thing Henry Jackson could have done was to start off with a loss somewhere. New Hampshire would have required a lot of candidate time, and an ability to attract very good people in the organization; and we didn't have much candidate time. Senator Jackson did not like going to New Hampshire too well, and so we didn't go there very often. By the December 1975 filing time, we did not have the option of going to New Hampshire because we hadn't done the necessary homework. There were two ways not to lose New Hampshire: one was to win it and the other was not to go in. The one sure way was not to go in, so we didn't. We applied the same basic reasoning to Iowa, deciding that it was a place that required substantial early candidate time which we couldn't give, and that we ought to do only those things we could do well.

DAVID S. BRODER (associate editor, *Washington Post*): Why didn't Wallace go to New Hampshire?

SNIDER: I asked him not to. I did not want him to get involved in anything until Florida. This was where we [Wallace people] started off in 1972, and I felt we had a chance of winning in Florida if we got in there early enough and did the things we needed to do. I was successful in keeping him out of New Hampshire, but I compromised on a visit to test the water in Massachusetts. He came up and had a couple of meetings in Massachusetts, got a large crowd, and didn't realize that he was meeting in much smaller rooms than he did in 1972; with five hundred people in a room that seated two hundred and fifty, it looked fantastic, especially with him sitting [in a wheelchair] instead of standing up. I kept telling him that I still thought he ought not to get involved in Massachusetts, but he kept talking about how even a third or fourth would be a victory, better than nothing at all. He was thinking about the school busing situation [in Boston], among other things, and how if he could kick off as the winner up there, this would put him back in the position he left off with in 1972. I was overruled by him personally on Massachusetts.

GABUSI: In the Udall campaign, we were concerned from the beginning with the question of whether it was a contest of issues or candidates. How should our candidate be projected? What was his constituency? In Florida, for instance, one ideological position came to be known as "anybody but Carter." We made a judgment that we wouldn't enter the Florida primary, even to pick up some districts in Dade County, where liberal progressives were importuning us to come in. We decided to let Jimmy Carter take a crack at Governor

Wallace, and that was an ideological judgment for the good of the country, or the good of the party, however you define it. On the other hand, we had a television piece showing our candidate's home town and pine trees, and him walking around the forests, that was pure candidate. Throughout the campaign we were in dispute about whether the candidate should be projected this way or through issues.

PERRY: Did the candidate participate in making decisions of this type?

QUINN: Udall was most frequently involved in the issue and image kinds of decisions and in strategic decisions to the extent that they involved significant financial consequences. He was not a submarine commander who would put one person in charge of one thing and let him run with it; he was more of a courtroom lawyer who wanted to hear from all sides, and let all the evidence come in, and arbitrate different views—which at times was awkward and time-consuming.

TUCHMAN: If Udall knew someone for a while, he would delegate enormous authority; but he had a real reluctance to delegate authority to someone whom he hadn't known and worked with. In a campaign with a vastly expanding circle, that was a problem.

POWELL: But to get back to the question of what's style and what's substance: I think people draw an artificial distinction between what's an issue and what's a nonissue. There was a tremendous yearning in the country this year for something of substance that you could put some faith in. This all followed the disillusionment with causes that start out in a blaze of glory and end in disappointment. People all over the land were looking for something they thought they had known once and somehow had lost touch with. I think that pine trees and home towns said something even to people who had never seen a small town, because they suggested something that they wanted. If we say that this is not an issue in this country, then we miss what's going on with people out there.

WATTENBERG: Jackson was running as a traditional values candidate too, but such things ultimately have a policy root as well—they are not just style. When we polled in Massachusetts, we were astonished to find that people's views on substantive issues, particularly foreign policy and defense, were very much in accord with what

Jackson stood for, and Massachusetts was allegedly the most liberal state in the union.

FRIEDMAN: In terms of Senator Bayh's candidacy, New Hampshire was very important in a lot of ways. As we got into the field and began collecting our polling data, the first thing we discovered was that, as of the first of January, Governor Carter had preempted the entire right half of the New Hampshire electorate, and everybody else was simply left to divide up the remaining 50 percent. We came into New Hampshire with severe handicaps in terms of finances and organization. While the Carter media, the radio at least, went on the air in New Hampshire the first or second week in January, at that point we had not even selected a media consultant and did not do so until after the Iowa caucus. Even after we had selected a media consultant, we had a problem in gathering funds to put the material on the air. Our view coming out of Iowa and into New Hampshire was a relatively optimistic one despite the organizational and financial drawbacks, but we discovered that we lacked the one crucial resource in New Hampshire—time. You can talk about New Hampshire in terms of local paid media and national free media, but in my view, New Hampshire is the paradigm of retail politicking—one to one, down the street, door to door, over the phone, day after day—and that required that the candidate spend time there. Governor Carter decided to spend a lot of time there, as did Congressman Udall. It was not that Senator Bayh decided not to spend much time in New Hampshire; it was that we never had much time to spend in New Hampshire. Senator Bayh did not even get there until late October [1975], at which time he was forced to allocate a lot of time to build the base we were hoping for in New York. We were looking down the road at New York. We expected not to win some of the early primaries, but we expected to continue to do well enough. We saw it as a game of musical chairs, in which after every primary somebody was going to be left standing up and have to get out of the game. We didn't expect that to be Senator Bayh.

Whenever Senator Bayh spent time in New Hampshire, things would improve. Our tracking surveys showed us moving up considerably on Congressman Udall in early February. We were moving a lot, but we could not take advantage of that because of our inability to get on the air—we had only a small radio program, practically no television, and no print media. As we analyzed them just after New Hampshire, the results showed that in every major city in New Hampshire with the exception of Nashua, Senator Bayh beat Congressman

Udall and finished a relatively strong second to Carter. The pattern of his votes very closely paralleled the pattern of where he traveled. Where he had time to do that retail campaigning, he built the coalition we were after, a combination of some liberal votes with a dollop of blue collar votes. Even in Manchester, where we had the most severe opposition of Mr. Loeb's *Union-Leader*, we finished a good strong second because the candidate had been able to spend time there. But all in all, coming out of New Hampshire, we were only barely alive, having finished third with 16 percent instead of the 20 percent we had hoped for. We were exhausted.

QUINN: In New Hampshire—really from Iowa right through Massachusetts—the labor vote was pretty much irrevocably taken out of Udall's reach by Bayh. And that had a long-range impact.

POWELL: It would be a mistake to interpret the Carter victory in New Hampshire as one in which the right wing united solidly behind one candidate and defeated a splintered left wing group of several candidates. If you go back and look at the exit polling, you'll see that we [Carter people] got almost exactly the same percentage of people who considered themselves liberals, of people who considered themselves moderates, and of people who considered themselves conservatives.

KEEFE: One last word about New Hampshire: I thought the Ford-Reagan battle was going to be the big story of the New Hampshire primary, and that the Democratic primary was going to be mushy, with a lot of guys finishing with not much, and so forth. In fact, the Reagan-Ford race never ended on election night; so the networks, in order to avoid making a mistake, said nothing about the Republicans other than the race was too close to call and gave Jimmy Carter the whole night. He had a tremendous halo in New Hampshire simply because the Republicans were too close to call.

PERRY: But what effect did New Hampshire have on Massachusetts, and Massachusetts on Florida? Why didn't Jackson's primary victory in Massachusetts have more effect in Florida?

WATTENBERG: After the Massachusetts primary, Jackson, unlike Carter, was not on the cover of *Time*; he was not on the cover of *Newsweek*; we did not get articles about his cousin who has a worm farm. And that was the story of the Jackson campaign for the next six weeks, and that was what I think killed that campaign. Jackson had won a totally unanticipated victory, beyond what the press had expected, in a state with ten times as many delegates as New Hampshire, and the effect was barely visible. We were dismayed.

RAFSHOON: Massachusetts was sandwiched in between what were perceived to be the two big primaries, New Hampshire and Florida. The only significance people saw in Jackson's Massachusetts victory was that Jackson might cut Carter in Florida, and help put him in second place there.

BLACK VOTE

BENJAMIN D. BROWN (deputy campaign director for Carter): What we really got to in Florida was a new dynamic, because that's where the black factor became a very significant element in the process. I think that was the important new dimension of the Carter candidacy. Our effort to organize the black vote in Florida started basically in October 1975. For the first time, black communities were being organized on a very systematic basis, rather than on the usual street money concept that had characterized most past efforts in black communities. Our greatest competition in Florida was the Jackson effort.

Historically, blacks have followed the national leadership, and we had a very strong movement among national leaders to have blacks go uncommitted—but I knew full well that that was a Hubert Humphrey movement. Our strategy was to develop our own network of people through a very low key operation. We started early; we went into communities and convinced leaders that they shouldn't be looking for great resources that might be coming down other channels, but should be taking this opportunity to select the candidate that the black vote could deliver to the nation. We got our first indication in Massachusetts that Jimmy Carter was selling to black communities: we pulled upwards of 40 percent of the black vote in Roxbury [part of Boston], which was a clear indication that there was a breakthrough in black communities in the North. I didn't have any doubt that we could organize black communities in the South. The question was percentage turnout, and we were very much amazed at the percentage turnout in the primaries in the South. Once we got voters out, Jimmy received 70 percent of their vote, much of the other 30 percent going to Scoop Jackson. Everybody had looked for the national established leadership to deliver the votes to the designee of the liberal wing of the party; we were not saying that Jimmy Carter was less than liberal, but he was a progressive who would provide a vehicle for establishing new black leadership.

SNIDER: Inadvertently, Governor Wallace helped Jimmy Carter with the black vote. The governor began to get the idea very early that his chief competitor was going to be Jimmy Carter, and he began to take some personal potshots at him, calling him by name. This was a strong indication to the black voter that one candidate's philosophy was opposed to the other candidate's philosophy. So, without meaning to, we were handing Carter the black vote.

Even though the polls never showed us as the winner in Massachusetts, the governor felt basically that he could win in that state. Had we won in Massachusetts, I think that Florida would have probably come in; but we didn't, and that reflected onto Florida. What we found in Florida was that people actually thought that George Wallace was going to win in Massachusetts, and they were disappointed when he didn't. But the biggest thing to hit us in Florida that we never expected at all, though we should have, was the health factor. A postelection poll showed that some three out of five people who had voted for him before did not vote for him this time because of his health, not because they doubted he would make the best candidate. Some of them said that it was unfair to him to put him into this awesome task of president in his physical condition. And of course, some of the opposition was using the health question very effectively too.

Then we made two important mistakes. We tried to dispel the health thing by keeping the governor on a very tough schedule. We told him that any time he felt it was too much, he should just say so; but being the type of political individual that he is, he would never say that anything was too much for him. Then right in the middle of all this, during a speaking trip, one of our six foot four inches, 300 pound troopers fell on top of him when they were getting him on the airplane and broke his leg. They carried him to the hospital, and David Dick [of CBS] did a fine stand-up in front of the hospital, reporting that the governor was in the operating room now and they didn't know his condition. The governor came out that night and had two rallies in Panama City, all with that broken leg in a cast sticking out on national press. When he got home that night, the first thing that the doctor had to do was carry him to the hospital and take the damn cast off, and David had another opportunity to stand in front of the local hospital. That hurt.

The other important mistake had to do with the independent vote. We had a small but hard core independent vote that was staying with George Wallace for one reason. They knew in the back of their minds that he would not get the Democratic nomination, but they were staying with him to keep him viable as a third party candidate. He got pressured a lot about this, and at one point he said absolutely under no circumstances would he run as a third party candidate, and that was the end of that. This turned off quite a few independents, who went to Governor Carter as an acceptable alternate to Governor Wallace. From that point on, we went down hill.

ELEANOR RANDOLPH (correspondent, *Chicago Tribune*): After Carter lost the Massachusetts primary, some of the Carter people said that they had never seen Governor Carter in such a foul mood; and the next day he did make several comments about Jackson's campaigning in Massachusetts.

WATTENBERG: During the period of the Massachusetts primary, there was an enormous amount of resentment against Carter by staff members of the various campaigns, who felt that he would come very close to short-circuiting the system if he were to win in Massachusetts. People from the camps of Udall, Bayh, and Shriver would come up to me in the Parker House in Boston and say quietly, "If it ever comes to a showdown between Jackson and Carter, we want to be counted in with Jackson because we have just had it with Carter, up to here."

POWELL: Had we [Carter people] won Massachusetts, by whatever stroke it would have taken to have done that, we certainly would have gone on to win in Florida. I think you can make a plausible theory that if that had happened, the "anybody but Carter" thing would have kicked off the day after Florida. We probably would have won the nomination anyway, because we would have gotten every Southern delegate; but it would have been a bloody process, and the Republicans would have been the beneficiaries. Instead of the South coming back to the party, to a large extent there would have been a heightened feeling of suspicion and paranoia.

SIEGEL: It seemed to me that the brokering strategy crumbled after Florida, in part because Birch Bayh fell apart too early and in part because there was no longer any expectation that Wallace was going to come into the convention with up to 700 delegates.

SUBSEQUENT STRATEGIES

PERRY: Who was left after Florida, going into Illinois [March 16]? What were the strategies for the next batch of primaries?

FRIEDMAN: You're talking about mid-March, and I think in mid-March there were two influences that shaped a lot of what happened.

First, this was just about the time, as a result of the Supreme Court decision and the inability to rework the law, that the matching money turned off for a little while. This development made absolutely paramount the differing abilities of the various remaining campaigns to manage their money and to find money. Second, it is essential to understand the relationship of each of the remaining candidates to the labor coalition clearinghouse operation.

ALAN L. OTTEN (correspondent, *Wall Street Journal*): As I recall, things had shaken down to Carter, Jackson, Udall. Why did the liberals, who were so effective in 1972, not at that point begin to coalesce behind Udall, who was clearly the most liberal among the three remaining? Was it the desire to win? Was it that people were hanging back for Humphrey? What was it that kept Udall from emerging successfully?

QUINN: There was no war—there was no moral imperative around that [Udall] candidacy. Had Scoop Jackson or George Wallace then been in the position of Jimmy Carter, the constituencies of the left would have gone to Udall because both Jackson and Wallace were identifiable "enemies" of those constituencies. Jimmy Carter was simply never anathema to the left. Besides this, as time went on, it became more and more a commonly held belief that Udall could never bring labor around in the way that Bayh or Jackson might—in late 1975 and early 1976, we were haunted by the 14B controversy.* And then we began to have problems with the black constituency.

WATTENBERG: There simply aren't enough liberals around to make that much of an impact. When Udall announced officially in New York that he was no longer a liberal and was now a progressive, the only other guy campaigning that announced he was a liberal was Jackson.

TUCHMAN: There was some coalescence in New York in that large numbers of key people from the Bayh organization joined the Udall campaign.

SIEGEL: I wonder whether Mo Udall, a Mormon from Arizona, was just the wrong person to coalesce an urban, liberal, black, labor coalition.

*In 1965, Congressman Udall voted against repeal of the "right-to-work" section (14B) of the Taft-Hartley law.

FRIEDMAN: When Senator Bayh dropped out after Massachusetts, some people who participated in his campaign, in New York particularly, moved into Udall's campaign; but there was a rather glaring exception to that—the senator himself. That was an indication that there was just not going to be a movement to Congressman Udall in 1976. There wasn't a moral imperative, and there was the tremendous desire on many people's part in our [Bayh's] organization that Congressman Udall not get the nomination.

QUINN: Winning in Massachusetts or New Hampshire was essential to any Udall victory. And while Udall was waiting for the New York and Wisconsin primaries to happen and hopefully result in some kind of coalescence, Carter was winning in Florida, North Carolina, and Illinois.

CADDELL: After Florida, there was one serious candidacy—Carter's —and everybody else, because the media had made it that way. The calendar was dictating that anyone who was in Carter's position in North Carolina [March 23] and Illinois [March 16] was going to be the serious candidate; and it was also dictating April 6—Wisconsin and New York—which would be the real Carter problem because of his stretched resources at this stage. If there was going to be a final shoot out, it was going to be in Pennsylvania [April 27]. There were three full weeks between New York and Pennsylvania, with no primaries in between. It would be the only period where there would be sustained attention.

WATTENBERG: Just prior to the New York primary, Governor Carter said that it was now a showdown between Jackson and Carter. Jackson won New York, and as of that night we [Jackson people] had run against Carter three times in three big states and won twice. I woke up the next morning in a hotel, and I think it was on the *Today* show that they said, "Well, it's now a showdown between Carter and Humphrey." I literally fell off the bed. Instead of it finally being a head to head clash between Jackson and Carter, it was still Carter versus the pack, and the pack then was Udall and Jackson, symbolized by Humphrey.

HART: Udall had to have Wisconsin if he was going to be the nominee. About two weeks before the primary, he was down by about 34 to 17 percent, Jackson had about 12 percent, Wallace had 8 or 9, and there was a huge undecided. We tried to modify the dynamic of the election, associate Carter with the status quo, and position Udall in terms of change. We went very, very hard with the media, and Mo picked up from about 17 percent to about 30 percent and was closing in on the final five days of the campaign. It was about 34 percent Carter, 30 percent Udall. We realized that we had to win Wisconsin or the ballgame would be over—but we came in second. Going into Pennsylvania, it didn't make any difference that we had done well in both New York and Wisconsin. We had not finished first in either.

SIEGEL: There never should have been a Wisconsin primary. That was the one case where the reform wing of the party totally reversed its position from 1972 and politicized the CRC [Compliance Review Commission] to lift the ban on an open primary. Udall came in, and there was a lot of liberal pressure on members of the CRC to give Udall a chance to win the Wisconsin primary.

QUINN: We [Udall people] did not orchestrate that effort. We were of the opinion that the Wisconsin primary should be held. I think it's unreasonable to have expected us to stand up and say, "We're good reformers, so let's throw out the Wisconsin primary," when we had been building an organization there for over a year.

SIEGEL: I just want to suggest that the reformers who screamed so much in 1972 about changing the rules in California didn't have any problem about changing them in Wisconsin.

GABUSI: The activists involved in the 1972 election were not necessarily the same group of activists who were interested in maintaining the Wisconsin primary in 1976. Different individuals were involved.

But to go on to the impact of finances in Wisconsin: [in the Udall campaign] we were not raising money of any significance there. We had the mail program, with a list of 38,000 plus that we could draw on—15 to 20 percent return every time. But that was the only income we had, and it had just been tapped out the weekend before the Wisconsin primary. We came out of Wisconsin with a $150,000 debt that had to be repaid by our incoming money, and we went into the Pennsylvania primary with only a $50,000 line of credit from one small agency. I am curious as to the line of credit that the Carter people had in the Pennsylvania primary.

CADDELL: The Udall people outspent the Carter people in Wisconsin by a fairly large amount of money. Our [Carter's] treasurer, Bob Lipshutz, made a very critical decision at this point. There was a tremendous amount of pressure for us to pour less money into New York and more into Wisconsin, because there was a fear of a double loss on April 6. But Lipshutz said that he was not going to spend the money, that he was going to hold back a reserve for Pennsylvania. So we just went with what we had in Wisconsin, and tried to hold on.

KEEFE: The Carter people managed their money better during that period, and in my opinion, this was decisive.

"FUZZINESS" ISSUE

OTTEN: In Pennsylvania during this period there was a gradual development of the "fuzziness" issue, the flip-flop, relating to Carter. How did the Carter people see this? Did the Jackson and Udall people see this as an opening?

CADDELL: Wisconsin was an important departure point in terms of voters' perceptions, and it was there that the flip-flop question started to cut. Then we began to see it in sizeable numbers afterward, in Pennsylvania. It was Carter against the field, and the voters were beginning to perceive Carter as a person who might well be president. The other candidates were not being perceived by the voters as real candidates, in the sense that they were likely to win the nomination. Pennsylvania was the first place we [Carter people] really confronted the fuzziness issue. We had to deal with it in order to stop the slippage in Pennsylvania.

RAFSHOON: There was a great deal of adverse publicity and anti-Carter advertising about Carter being fuzzy on the issues; but from the beginning, our [Carter's] advertising had been probably more issue-oriented than that of any of the other candidates. We did emphasize character and values in our advertising, but we also had quite a bit on issues. We had Jimmy Carter speaking on a variety of issues in sixty second spots—generalized, of course. I could show you a script of radio time in New Hampshire when he talked about government mismanagement. When he talked about an Arab boycott during the debates, people said this was news, but we had been using that in our advertising as far back as Iowa. In the Pennsylvania primary, we found that by getting on the air earlier than Udall and Jackson, who by that time were using a lot of anti-Carter advertising, we could manage to defuse the fuzziness charge. We ran the same type of advertising in Pennsylvania as we had earlier, but we labeled it as issues.

GABUSI: The Udall campaign was not running anti-Carter advertising in Pennsylvania, but Mo was speaking directly to that question daily. Our advertising was very limited.

RAFSHOON: Carter was on for five days before Udall's first ad, and fortunately, we got on before a holiday weekend. By the time Udall tried to buy media, the stations were closed, and he couldn't get on.

KEEFE: Jackson got 20 percent of the vote in Pennsylvania, Udall got 19 percent, and Carter won a large victory with 37 percent. What was the impact of that victory?

HART: At that stage, it appeared to all the pros that the ballgame was over. And yet at the same time, it appeared to me that the Carter campaign was doggedly pursuing the same strategy, and taking unnecessary risks in Maryland [May 18], Michigan [May 18], and Nebraska [May 11]. At one point, Carter was running in six primaries in one day. Why did he continue to take on everybody?

POWELL: For one thing, there were some fairly serious mistakes made [in the Carter campaign]. For instance, everybody thought Carter ought to go into Maryland, and so we did it—but it was a dumb thing to do and almost cost us Michigan. We recognized the potential for havoc that resided in the candidacy of Governor Brown, and we thought we had a chance to nip it in the bud in Maryland. But obviously, what we did was just the opposite; we gave him a boost by giving him a contested state. But other than such mistakes, we just didn't think it was locked up—the delegates weren't there. We looked at this process as delegate accumulation, and we believed that we really had to have the delegates by the time the thing was over or there was a chance that it could slip away from us.

POTENTIAL HUMPHREY CAMPAIGN

SIMON: I agree that the delegate count was not there for Carter, at least from what we were calculating on the Humphrey side. We had an informal group that was going through an up and down process on a potential campaign for Humphrey. At one point, for example, [Minnesota Congressman] Bob Bergland and I had prepared a letter that was going to go out to ten or fifteen thousand former delegates and Democratic officials, and then we got a call from Senator Humphrey saying that we shouldn't send it. We backed off, and we didn't send the letter out. Then there was another understanding that Humphrey would authorize an organization that Bob Short from Minneapolis had put together, whereby a committee would explore the possibility of a candidacy. We pulled in people from all over the country for this committee, and we were ready to make an announcement when Senator Humphrey asked us not to do it. Then Joe Crangle [Democratic chairman of Erie County (N.Y.)] and I got a few others together and said, "We simply have to form an organization, and if Humphrey calls us and asks us not to do it, we're going to go ahead and do it anyway." And so that got things going.

At that point, there were five primaries left: New Jersey, Nevada, Idaho, Oregon, and Nebraska. We had a poll showing that if Humphrey should become a candidate, he would beat Carter 72 percent to 17 in New Jersey [June 8]. We had a poll showing him winning in Nebraska and Oregon [May 25]; we had no feel for what would happen in Nevada [May 25], and we assumed we would lose Idaho [May 25]. But it sounded to us like a reasonably good shot if we could get Humphrey to go. At this point, everybody knew that this decision was building, and a meeting was scheduled for about five o'clock Wednesday afternoon. Because I had a fundraiser, I was not able to be there. After the five o'clock meeting, he called me at my fundraiser and said, "I'm going to go home and have a bowl of soup with my lady, but I don't think I'm going to be a candidate." Then about midnight, I got a call from Neal Peterson [a former aide], who is very close to Humphrey, saying that I should call Humphrey at the apartment first thing in the morning. I called him at eight o'clock Thursday morning at his apartment and he said, "I talked to Muriel and the kids last night and they encouraged me to go on, and I'm going to be a candidate. Can you get a crowd and get some of your colleagues to be at the press conference?" I said we would start on it. Things were really rolling fast; and then at eleven o'clock, I got a call from Dave Gartner, Humphrey's administrative assistant, saying the decision had been reversed. We were to have the press conference [on April 29] at one-thirty, and he said to come and meet with Humphrey at one. About eight of us went to meet with Muriel and Humphrey. Humphrey said, "I know all of you don't agree with this decision, but it's my decision." And Mondale said, "If you think that's the right decision, then it's the right decision."

MOE: Those twenty-four hours following the Pennsylvania primary results were very hectic. I was in the five o'clock Wednesday meeting Paul Simon referred to; about a dozen people were there, and with only a couple of exceptions, they urged him strongly to get into the New Jersey primary. The filing for New Jersey was the next day.

Unlike most of his friends, I had become convinced after he decided not to go into the primaries early that it made no sense for him to go in at any later date, particularly at this point, because he had no money and no organization. Some of us were convinced that even if he won New Jersey, it wouldn't change the ultimate outcome, and he might be humiliated in the process. But he went around the room, and he asked everybody two questions. First he asked, "What should I do?" and most people urged him to run. Then he asked, "What would you do if you were me?" and a few people changed their answers on that. What struck me about the whole thing was the finality of the Thursday press conference. Humphrey never intended his statement at that press conference to be a final statement in terms of his no longer being available for the nomination, and yet that's precisely the impression that came out of it—I think unintentionally.

SIEGEL: People would laugh about Humphrey's indecision—first he was running and then he was not running—but it was not funny. He was under intense pressure to go in from labor, from blacks, from mayors, from the power centers of the Democratic party. Some of us felt that maybe he was under pressure from people who held their self-interest before his; and I think he had this in the back of his mind at all times as well, although he would never articulate it that way. The night before his decision, I spoke with him for a long time, and he asked, "Won't people think . . . ? Won't the press say . . . ? Won't they bring up this, won't they bring up that?" And he asked me finally, "What do you think I should do?" And I said, "This is like asking someone to play Russian roulette with somebody else's head, and I'm not going to do it." And he said, "There's something about this that's wrong—I can't tell you what it is, but there's something in my gut that's telling me 'no,' and I don't think I should get into this." Yet he spent the whole half hour conversation looking for justification to get in. He was very ambivalent.

SIMON: There has been a lot of speculation about whether his health was a factor in all this. I don't think it was. He had just had a physical, and every indication was that he was in great shape.

KEEFE: The Jackson campaign was in the process of some major decisionmaking at that time in terms of what we were going to do. After Pennsylvania, it was clear that we were not going to have enough delegates to win on the first ballot, and Jackson decided that it was not his role to try and make it a brokered convention. He was somewhat interested in helping Humphrey at that point, and there were indirect communications between the two senators that were sort of confused. So finally I was asked to call Humphrey and communicate what was really happening in the Jackson meetings. I gave him my report, and he said, "Keefe, did you read the *Washington Post* this morning?" And I said, "Yes, sir, I did." He said "Have you read the editorials?" And I said, "No, I haven't." So he read the last two paragraphs of an editorial which basically made all the negative points about a Humphrey candidacy—why should Humphrey jump into the open arms of the people who just dropped Scoop Jackson in Pennsylvania, he's only serving as a spoiler, and that sort of thing. And he read me that and asked me what I thought they were saying. I said, "It seems to me that they're saying you shouldn't run."

BRODER: Did Carter or any of his people attempt to influence Humphrey's decision?

POWELL: I don't doubt that there may have been some people with some degree of closeness who might have spoken with some view toward Jimmy in their minds too; but I don't think we [Carter people] had any lines out, because there was very little chance of our exerting any real influence. We thought that if Humphrey entered the race, it would be a damn bloody fight which we would probably end up winning. There's no doubt in my mind that Jimmy had already convinced himself that Humphrey was going to run and that psychologically he was geared up for it and ready to go. Jimmy had accepted the prospect of an extremely bloody, tough battle right down to the end of this thing, and I think there was a tremendous emotional release when we got the news of Humphrey's decision. What you have to keep in mind as you think about Humphrey's position at this time is that if you're going to win a nomination, you have to have delegates. If you're going to get delegates, you've got to run and win. If you run and win, people are going to start beating you about the head and ears, and enough of that and you're going to start bleeding. That happened to us, it happened to everybody, and only under the most fortuitous of circumstances do you get there without going through that.

LATE PRIMARIES

PERRY: Moving past Pennsylvania, with a cast of Carter, Church, Brown, and uncommitted, certain problems began to occur for the Carter people in the final series of primaries.

POWELL: By that point, Carter was the one candidate running that people thought might actually end up in the White House, and so he was taking blows with increasing frequency as we went along. It became increasingly clear in our polls that people who weren't sure that they wanted Carter as the Democratic nominee and as president were feeling more comfortable voting for someone else. Also, our "run everywhere" strategy was beginning to take its toll of our resources and physical endurance. We made fundamental mistakes in Maryland and Nebraska. We had to face Governor Brown and Senator Church, two people coming in late who had not been scarred up; and we had to face them in Western primaries, where we were not well known and therefore were more vulnerable to personal attack.

OTTEN: Did the Carter people ever feel that all the opposition attacks—from Jackson in Pennsylvania, Udall in Ohio and Michigan, Brown in New Jersey and Maryland—got over the line into the unfair category, or did you think they were within the rules of the political game?

POWELL: Of course, I basically felt that any attack was unfair . . . but beyond that, it's probably exactly what I would have done had I been in their position. Being attacked is part of the price you pay if you're going to run. It balances out. Brown couldn't win the nomination because he started late and couldn't get enough delegates. But he benefited from starting late in that he was never subjected to much scrutiny at all. If he had started early, he would have gotten a pretty thorough going over just as we did; and by the end of the thing, he would have been limping a bit too.

HART: After Pennsylvania, Udall was really down and out. A poll was taken in Michigan at that stage which showed Carter at 52 percent and Udall at 19 percent. Carter's support broke down this way: 21 percent was strong support and 31 percent was weak. So there were a lot of people voting for him who had reservations: almost half of his weak supporters agreed that he was fuzzy on the issues and that he was all things to all people; likewise, some agreed that he was a nice guy but were not sure he had the necessary ability. When we looked at everything in terms of Udall and where he was, it seemed to be necessary to go negative in order to make a competitive situation. If you went back and asked Mo if he ran a negative campaign in Wisconsin or prior to Wisconsin, I think he'd tell you he definitely did not. But when we met to discuss Michigan, there was a definite decision that both media and candidate would go negative because it was the only way left.

POWELL: That sort of strategy probably meant that even though Udall just might shoot us [Carter] down, there was very little chance that he was going to profit from it. But it probably was your only shot.

GABUSI: After Pennsylvania, Udall believed that his own chance of getting the nomination was almost zero. The question was whether the process was going to continue and allow someone other than Carter to pull it together. Udall needed to decide whether keeping that option open was important enough for him to continue to do what had to be done. If he wanted to keep the option open, he had to go on with a negative operation in Michigan. And it almost worked.

BRODER: How much is there to the theory that what really made Michigan tight was the first case of backlash against Carter's very visible black support.

BROWN: In support of Carter, Coleman Young [mayor of Detroit] started a negative campaign and picked up on the Mormon issue, which is a very sensitive issue with blacks in this country.* The issue had been there all along, but it was not exploited until the Michigan primary; and there might have been a white backlash against Coleman Young's activities.

CADDELL: But that wasn't the problem for Carter in Michigan: the problem in Michigan was the crossover factor. There was a tremendous Ford campaign to draw crossovers, even ads on black radio, trying to get votes against Reagan. As we tracked that, we found that 13 or 15 percent of the people who said they were going to vote in the Democratic primary said they might also consider voting in the Republican primary; and these people were three to one Carter voters. During the weekend before the primary, we began to see them move. Early on, we had about a forty-eight to thirty lead, but by Sunday night we were finding that eight points of that forty-eight were defecting to the Republican primary. By reinterviewing the respondents from Thursday, Friday, and early Saturday, we could see that those Democrats now moving to vote in the Republican primary were previous Carter voters by better than four to one. Thus, Udall was actually moving very little, voters were leaving Carter to vote for Ford, and the margin was closing rapidly. The very early crossovers

*The Mormon church excludes blacks from its priesthood.

had gone to Reagan; these later ones were all Ford crossovers. If you look at the results in Michigan, you'll see that there were more votes cast for Gerald Ford than were cast for all the Democrats combined.

TUCHMAN: Do you have any information on where the 1972 Wallace votes [in Michigan] went?

CADDELL: They were split up by 1976. Some went to the Republican primary, Carter got the plurality of them, and Udall got some.

OTTEN: How early did the Carter people perceive that they had a problem with the Catholic ethnic voters?

CADDELL: Though we had had trouble in terms of the percentage of Catholics we were carrying—particularly in urban areas—in places like Illinois, the religious split between Protestants and Catholics really showed up in Maryland. Part of Catholics' response to Carter seemed to stem from a sense of unfamiliarity with him, an uneasiness that came more from style than from substance. But also, he was never very strong on some of the issues that had to do particularly with Catholics. This was already a problem with us by late May, when we started looking at the general election.

FINAL CHALLENGERS

PERRY: What was Brown's strategy in his very late start?

KANTOR: On March 12, when Governor Brown announced to three reporters in his office, there obviously wasn't what you might call a game plan. There was no staff, no money, no campaign, no strategy, no list of primaries, no list of how you file. I was called by Jerry Brown on March 17 and started on March 21; and when we opened the office on April 21, fourteen filing dates had already passed since the time we announced. Brown announced because he thought that what he was articulating in California was not being articulated nationally and that it was fairly potent stuff. There had been a tremendous public reaction to his interview on *60 Minutes* and then the *Playboy* interview—the numbers and the kinds of letters were fantastic. We made our move right after Florida, prior to Wisconsin and New York and Pennsylvania, and prior to Hubert Humphrey's dropping out of the process. It looked as if Frank Church was going to be in the process, Mo Udall might win Wisconsin, and Scoop Jackson could win New York and Pennsylvania. In such a fractionated process, it seemed possible that a young governor coming out of California and winning maybe one primary outside California might be in a good position.

BRODER: Did Brown really misperceive his reputation in the Democratic party to the point that he thought he could be picked in a brokered convention?

KANTOR: It seemed clear to us that if he ran in a few primaries and was perceived nationally, he would rapidly rise in the polls. I think that was borne out by what happened. I see politics as just luck and timing and a lot of things that happen to you which you may or may not take advantage of; if you're there and you have a rising popularity and you have done well in some primaries, then you are as likely to be chosen as anybody else.

When it became clear that Governor Carter was going to win Pennsylvania, Governor Brown defined our strategy in terms of how we could change the chemistry of the race. We decided to go into Maryland, to start thinking about Oregon, to do something about Rhode Island [June 1]; and we hoped that Hubert Humphrey was going to enter the process. The day after Pennsylvania, we left for Maryland, and the next day Hubert Humphrey stated that he was not going to be in the race. At that point, what we needed was every break in the world—a miracle. We decided to concentrate on Maryland and try to figure out some strategy that might be successful. We sent people to Nevada, where we were on the ballot; and we began to talk to people in New Jersey, who were at that point uncommitted but really pledged to Hubert Humphrey. As we worked in Maryland, we hoped that Mo Udall could win in Michigan and that Frank Church would win a number of Western states, and that the process would continue to be fractionated. Our biggest fear was that Carter wouldn't run against us in Maryland. That would have been devastating to any pretensions we had; and even if we had won a victory, it would have been of no importance whatsoever. We would have just gone back to California and tried to hold our place. Although it seemed to some that it was over, it seemed to us as we talked to delegates—Jackson delegates, Wallace delegates, uncommitted delegates—that it was not over.

CADDELL: When Jerry Brown arrived in Maryland, he made a big impact. By the beginning of the next week, Carter had fallen behind Brown in our polls. Some of us half thought of not going to Maryland, but Jimmy said that he was behind in the polls already and he didn't plan to lose the state.

HAMILTON JORDAN (campaign manager for Carter): When I first heard that Brown was coming to Maryland, I thought it was crazy. But after a few days, I realized that it was a state with a large Catholic vote and that a disproportionate number of the suburban voters were employed by the federal government and were probably frightened by Carter's reorganization policy and the anti-Washington statements. There was a machine in Baltimore and other areas of the state that Governor Brown had already captured. My initial impression was that we were going to cream Brown, but after a week, it seemed like a very sound strategy for Brown to have launched his campaign there. But even though Maryland and Michigan were not high points of the campaign, we still got delegates. It was never our strategy to duck a fight, and we won more than we lost.

PERRY: What was Senator Church's strategy at this point?

CURTIN: Senator Church had considered the possibility of running in some of the early primaries, but had decided against doing so. His final timetable called for him to go into Idaho, Oregon, and Rhode Island, and then California [June 8], on the assumption that Governor Brown would not campaign in California and that there would be no front runner. If he were successful in those four primaries, that would make a strong impression on people going into the convention. Senator Church never thought that he would be the beneficiary of any brokered convention, but we knew that there were people holding, particularly in case Humphrey might run. We had very good information about delegates, sometimes sooner than any of the other candidates, and knew that there was uncertainty among delegates. There also seemed to be regional advantages that strengthened Senator Church's candidacy. But the entry of Governor Brown and the resulting realization that we didn't have a chance in California turned the whole thing around.

PERRY: Did the Carter people see these final challenges as a Humphrey operation?

POWELL: We felt that Senator Humphrey was probably the only person who could ultimately benefit from them, other than Jerry Ford, but I don't think we wasted a lot of time worrying about who's in charge of who.

CARTER FOR SURE

PERRY: When did you think that you finally had a firm grasp on the nomination?

POWELL: It was the morning after the Ohio primary [June 9], when I got a call from Plains saying that Governor Carter had had a call from Governor Wallace. Then the next morning, there were the conversations with Jackson and Daley [mayor of Chicago]. I figured we finally had it.

SNIDER: As for the Wallace call: things had come to a point where it was ridiculous for us [Wallace people] to continue to suggest that we had a shot at the nomination, whether or not it might be a brokered convention. Also, Governor Wallace was concerned that Senator Humphrey might get the nomination. So as far as he could see, it was a matter of his choosing between Governor Carter and a Republican.

HART: Did the Carter people expect, after Florida, that Governor Wallace would eventually throw in his lot with them?

JORDAN: After we defeated Wallace in Florida, we felt we could probably defeat him in the other Southern states and carry the bulk of the Southern delegates. If Wallace had stayed neutral, or even if he had come out in favor of Humphrey as a candidate, I don't think he could have prevented his delegates, who for the most part were concentrated in the South, from supporting us. The choice was either a fellow Southerner, Jimmy Carter, or Humphrey, or one of the guys who came in at the end. There really was no good alternative to Carter.

SNIDER: I think the majority of the Wallace delegates would have gone with Carter. After Governor Wallace's endorsement of Carter, I had the task of actually calling and talking to each one of our delegates, about one hundred and sixty of them. Of these, only about fifteen—from Florida—objected to giving their votes to Carter. Governor Wallace had had all this in mind, but he made his final decision on the endorsement very abruptly. He hoped to close the door on Senator Humphrey, and hoped that if he endorsed Carter, others would do the same. He said that this was the time to do it, not tomorrow or the next day. So he made his decision. He operates very abruptly sometimes.

BRODER: The other key figure who threw in fast was Mayor Daley.

JORDAN: Mayor Daley had a basic political interest in electing Governor Carter. He had seen Carter do well in the southern part of his state, and he felt that Carter would help Illinois better than any other of the viable candidates. Also, the governor had paid the proper deference to Mayor Daley along the way, and had made courtesy calls on him. And of course, Illinois was one of two states in the country where we did not field delegates everywhere—we did not run against the Daley delegates in the city of Chicago. Along the way, I think Daley and Carter developed a respect and a relationship. Carter was by May the most viable candidate, the best candidate for the national party, and the best candidate for the ticket in Illinois. So when Carter won the Ohio primary, and then Governor Wallace made his statement, it was a natural thing that Daley would follow up with his. Also, Senator Jackson told Governor Carter that he could say that they had talked, and that Jackson expected his delegates to go to Carter.

PERRY: At this point, what was left of the "anybody but Carter" movement?

SNIDER: There was no nationally attractive alternative to Jimmy Carter, and the people who would have had to get it all together to stop Carter just had no heart to do it.

KEEFE: There was a growing respect for Carter. Even had Humphrey gone in, many of the Jackson delegates would have gone for Carter, just on ideological grounds. Everybody was saying that there would be an automatic transfer from being Jackson delegates to being Humphrey delegates, but this was not necessarily so.

PERRY: After June 8, the last primary day, Carter had 1,018 delegates, and the other candidates began to withdraw. The next step was the convention.

SELECTION OF MONDALE

BRODER: The one obvious question about the convention is, why Mondale? If the Democratic convention had not been dominated by the people who were actually there, would Carter still have chosen Mondale to be the vice presidential candidate? Was that the choice necessary to unite the party and get the hell out of the convention without any damage?

JORDAN: I think that the convention had very little, if anything, to do with Carter's decision to select Mondale. If you look at Carter's political behavior over a long period of time, you see that when given a choice, he usually does the bold thing. It would have been very comfortable and safe to have chosen [Maine Senator] Ed Muskie or possibly [Ohio Senator] John Glenn, and it was bold to go with Mondale. We realized that the choice of Mondale might create some problems for us in the South, but we thought it would also extend the appeal of the ticket. Muskie, Church, and Glenn would all have been satisfactory candidates; but Carter liked Mondale, he felt comfortable with him personally, he thought he was bright, and he saw him strengthening the ticket in the fall.

BRODER: Was the choice of Mondale an effort to head off [independent candidate] Gene McCarthy?

POWELL: Our discussions about the vice presidency didn't focus a great deal on that sort of consideration. There were obviously a number of constraints that limited our choices; but once we started to deal with the people inside those bounds, the long talks [at Carter's home] in Plains [Georgia] served as the key to the decision.

JORDAN: We ran a national poll—an ill-conceived idea—to test the acceptability of individual people and types of people for the vice presidency. We had a mayor on the list, a governor, women, blacks. Of all the people who had any name recognition at all in the country, Mondale did the poorest in that poll. My political concern about Mondale was whether his reputation as a political liberal would hurt us in the South. But if there was anything we could do to jeopardize our situation in the South, we were in bad shape anyway. I thought that it was worth the risk in the South to widen the appeal of the ticket elsewhere. Mondale had close ties with elements of the party that we had been estranged from—the labor movement, for example. He was a very attractive candidate.

SNIDER: Governor Wallace's endorsement further solidified Carter's position as a conservative in the South, and also helped make Mondale acceptable there. But the governor's endorsement had a negative impact on Carter's strength in other parts of the country, and Mondale served to offset that negative effect.

JORDAN: Before Governor Carter decided on Mondale and immediately afterwards, when there was some adverse reaction from the South, we said, "Look, for one hundred years now, the Democratic party has picked someone from another part of the country and then tried to placate us with someone from the South for vice president.

Jimmy's from the South, and you know him, and we have to reach out now and select someone having a slightly different ideology." That argument worked quite effectively.

BRODER: Did Mondale try to do anything to influence Carter's choice?

MOE: Shortly after the Humphrey decision following the Pennsylvania primary, the Mondale people thought about the possibility of a Carter-Mondale match. But we did almost nothing about it until Charlie Kirbo started making his rounds and possible vice presidential names kept bubbling up. According to Governor Carter's description at the convention, Mondale started off quite low on all the lists but kept surviving the cuts and eventually emerged on the final list. The session in Plains was the most determinative factor in the decision. I don't know what Carter and Mondale said there exactly, but the chemistry clicked between the two of them. Mondale prepared for the session by trying to conceptualize his view of the vice presidency and how it would relate to what Carter was interested in doing as president and what he himself might do as vice president. We spent several days talking that through, and he went down to Plains prepared to talk about it.

POWELL: Jimmy knew most of the people that he ended up talking to in Plains, but even the ones he knew best he didn't know very well. He had a fairly shallow sort of simplistic, stereotyped image of those people until he got into the Plains sessions. There was some feeling that the whole business was a bit of a charade, but it really was not that at all. He placed a great deal of importance on those sessions.

JORDAN: Jimmy told me that Mondale was able to quote back verbatim his position on the issues, and he was impressed that Mondale was serious about the interview and was prepared for it. Also, he found very few differences between them. The preparation and the Plains interview were both a big plus for Mondale. He started off toward the bottom of the governor's list, and as the thing developed, he looked better and better. The time that the governor took to make the decision was critical to the selection of Mondale.

JOHNSON: Prior to the time that Mondale went to Plains, Carter and Mondale had only seen each other on three previous occasions. We went down to Atlanta in 1974, when Mondale was exploring the possibility of running for president, and spent about forty-five min-utes one afternoon in the governor's office in what was basically a courtesy call. I think there had been two other meetings, probably five minutes long, so they had spent less than an hour together be-fore Mondale went to Plains.

ROLE OF LABOR, BLACKS, AND PARTY LEADERS

BRODER: Looking back over this whole nomination process, we have not really talked about the role of organized labor. How did labor play in this game, and how was this different from past selec-tion processes?

KEEFE: The AFL—CIO itself maintained its customary neutrality, to Jackson's detriment, I thought. However, one labor coalition com-prised of several unions with more progressive directors began early on with a strategy that was directed toward a brokered convention, and it rather aggressively sought delegates. The rest of the unions did not aggressively seek delegates to the convention, although a number of other labor delegates were elected, so the labor coalition was the major labor force in this whole act. The Jackson campaign had trouble dealing with the labor coalition, since the coalition was seen as the enemy by the established leadership of the AFL—CIO, and we thought that our long-term interests lay with the established leader-ship. We negotiated very poorly with the labor coalition; I think the Carter people negotiated best with it. The labor coalition people in Florida were very anti-Wallace, and the Carter people sold them the bill of goods of "let's knock off Wallace once and for all." They had a working relationship at least until the late stages, when the 14B problem came up.

SIEGEL: Not only was the labor coalition very effective in electing delegates, but when those delegates got to the convention, they were very cohesive and could be delivered. It seemed to me that they were taking positions contrary to Carter only to demonstrate just how cohesive and deliverable and active a force these several hundred delegates were.

BRODER: Again looking back overall, what was different or signifi-cant about the role of blacks in this selection process as compared to previous times?

BROWN: The significant difference [in the Carter campaign] was that there was involvement coming up from the bottom instead of just being at the top. Traditionally, there have been national leaders who could pretty much dictate the direction of the black vote in any given community. But this time around, the established black leadership didn't know what struck it. There was a tremendous organizing effort on the part of people who wanted to break away from the old pattern, and these people were local leaders, local legislators and councilmen. Blacks were volunteering, giving up time and money to the effort, and there was a pride this year that I had not seen in 1968 and 1972. Out of all this is coming a whole new cadre of leaders that you'll be hearing about in the next eight years or so. There was a feeling during this process on the part of blacks at the grassroots level that blacks were actually playing a significant part in the overall effort. We had people in the background like Jesse Hill and Herman Russell, very wealthy men who were part of the initial group of Georgians who seeded the campaign. We could talk about them, and we could point to different levels of our campaign structure where blacks were actually playing significant roles that transcended racial responsibility areas. That was a very significant factor; it surprised people because Jimmy was a Southerner, and it showed a whole new Southern thing.

POWELL: There are other folks [in the Carter campaign] who haven't been mentioned. We had an excellent group of people numbering several hundred or so, mostly from Georgia, who traveled into crucial states for us and did canvassing. They gave us the initial boost in New Hampshire. At the first of the year, a couple hundred of them went up and canvassed in the snow without any hats or gloves. They hit some 60 or 70 percent of the Democratic households up there within a week. They won New Hampshire for us, and they were largely responsible for our holding on to Wisconsin and perhaps Michigan too. We couldn't have done it without those folks out there pounding the pavement for us, and most of them were not really political types.

JORDAN: We [Carter people] eventually realized that a presidential primary is a spectator sport in New Hampshire, and it's difficult to get people from New Hampshire involved in and excited by their own damn primary. But the novelty of people paying their own way from Georgia received great local press. Every night when they finished their rounds, these people would write letters to all the people they had met that day—about 10,000 letters in all—and that helped us win New Hampshire.

BRODER: What about the role of party leaders in these proceedings?

SIEGEL: State chairmen, including some Southerners, were generally hostile to Carter through the primary process. Governors were a real problem. Jimmy in some ways ran against Congress and did not have a congressional background, so there was no relationship there. But when there was talk of an "anybody but Carter" movement, most people didn't have the stomach for it. Maybe this was a result of 1972; maybe it was based on a sense that we had to win and that we could win with this candidate. Maybe some of the state chairmen and governors and congressmen felt that Carter wouldn't be their personal choice if they had to pick the next president, but that he was a better candidate than anyone else running. At any rate, by the time of the convention, the state chairmen and governors and congressmen were very constructive. If Humphrey had made another decision, of course, or if one of the primaries had turned out differently, or if it was a really brokered race, then these party leaders probably would have gone for the brokering and probably would have worked pretty hard against the Carter candidacy.

SIMON: Among elected officials, I think there was a lack of enthusiasm for Carter, but there was not a great depth of hostility. The conversion was a relatively easy one. I don't know of any Democratic members of Congress who weren't out beating the bushes for the Carter candidacy.

KEEFE: There was a big difference between 1972 and 1976. In 1972, the hostility from the party leadership was somewhat well earned by the nominee [Senator George McGovern] in that his people at the local level tried to take over the party in addition to winning the delegates. In 1976, I don't know of any place that Carter people openly contested party chairmanships or that kind of thing. Carter was out to win the presidency, and McGovern was out to win the party.

ROBERT M. TEETER (director of research for Ford): Listening to all this discussion, I've noticed that the Carter people have talked about how, when they went into a state, they had to win it, they had to come out first. At no point were they thinking about staying alive, or finishing second everywhere overall, or getting 20 percent everywhere. It seems to me to be important to keep sight of the fact that the name of the game here is to win, to get more votes than anybody else in these primaries, and that's what they did. The perception of who had won the last two or three primaries was the important perception in the public's mind. It didn't matter who had four hundred delegates, or who finished second three times, or even if somebody had more delegates at one point than Carter. It was always perceived that he was the winner because he was winning the primaries; this idea of who was getting closest in the delegate count early on was not important. Who won each Tuesday was the important perception, and all the other strategies didn't matter.

✳ *Chapter 3*

The General Election

"Rose Garden" Strategy. Ford's Strategic Considerations. Development of Ford Campaign. Carter's Strategy. Southern Vote. Carter Campaign Organization. Reagan-Ford Relationship. Voters' Perceptions of Candidates. Ford Media Campaign. Carter Media Campaign. Impact of Debates. Role of Vice Presidential Candidates. McCarthy Candidacy. Importance of National Party Organizations. Critical Factors in Carter Win. Impact of Campaign Finance Law. Importance of Issues.

"ROSE GARDEN" STRATEGY

ELEANOR RANDOLPH (correspondent, *Chicago Tribune*): To start now with discussion of the general election, I'd like to ask Mike Duval to talk about the development of the Republican strategy before the Republican convention, when President Ford's "Rose Garden" strategy was formulated.

MICHAEL DUVAL (special counsel to Ford): About June 9, Jim Connor [White House staff secretary], Foster Channock [assistant to Richard Cheney], and I had lunch and talked about the campaign. It appeared to us that we had no political strategy at all, and that if the president got the nomination in August, he was going to need one. As a result of that lunch discussion, I wrote a memorandum dated June 11 that outlined what we called the "no campaign" strategy. The memorandum analyzed the possible negative impact of the president's campaigning in a political and partisan way. It went into some detail about the perceived strengths of Governor Carter and the perceived weaknesses of the president, and it outlined a campaign strategy after the nomination which would involve no active campaigning at all by the president—he would turn back funds to the treasury, issue a challenge for a series of four debates, and so forth. On the basis of that brief initial memorandum, a very small working group developed a 120 page memo that went through about eight different drafts. This memo was completed by the end of July, was approved by the president by the second week of August, and became the basic strategy paper for the fall election.

JAMES M. NAUGHTON (correspondent, *New York Times*): Was the essence of that strategy to change the nature of Ford's campaign style, to make him a different kind of candidate than he had been all his life, through Congress and the primaries?

ROBERT M. TEETER (director of research for Ford): Our campaign is often described as having gone reasonably well in the general election and very badly in the primaries, and the one single most important difference was the change in the president's behavior and his attitude toward the campaign. We had found in the primaries that when the president campaigned regularly, he was not effective. When he went out on the stump, his inexperience as a campaigner showed up. Throughout a day of five or six speeches, he would tend to get more strident and more partisan and harder on the attack; and when people began to see him this way on the evening news every night, his national approval ratings tapered off. Then when he'd stay in the White House for three or four months, he'd come back a little bit in the national polling. Of course, his campaigning would help him in the immediate areas that he was going through, but the general effect of it was negative. So this was the basis for the campaign strategy in the general election, the Rose Garden strategy. The president simply did better in communicating with the voters when he was perceived as the president, not as a candidate for president. I think that any president would probably do better as president than as a candidate, but it had to be doubly or triply true with President Ford because he's a very, very poor stump speaker.

NAUGHTON: To the extent that this strategy conflicted heavily with the way Ford had conducted himself for twenty years, how much difficulty was there persuading him to adopt this strategy?

TEETER: There may have been some difficulty in getting ready to persuade him, but it was not hard to go in and have a frank discussion with him about his candidacy.

DUVAL: You could go in there and level with him rather brutally. But what we were proposing called for change not only in his perception of the candidacy and how to run a campaign, but also the whole White House decisionmaking apparatus. There were some very painful decisions that would have to flow from an acceptance of this basic strategy. It wasn't easy to present the whole package in a way that was comprehensive and honest and didn't turn him off before he got through it.

FORD'S STRATEGIC CONSIDERATIONS

ALAN L. OTTEN (correspondent, *Wall Street Journal*): The Ford campaign strategy was based on certain assumptions drawn from your polling data—where you could hit Carter, what you could sell Ford on.

TEETER: There were two kinds of considerations: first, some conclusions we drew ourselves about the strengths and weaknesses of the president as a campaigner; second, the perceived differences between the candidates as shown by our polling data. The second group of considerations was the most important in our discussions with the president and in our campaign planning after the convention.

About the time of the Pennsylvania primary [April 27], we began to have the feeling that Governor Carter was going to be the opponent, and so we did a quick after-election study of the Pennsylvania primary to get a feel for what his appeal was and what kinds of people were supporting him and what people opposed him for. With the data from that poll, we compared the normal vote pattern in a Democratic primary with how each demographic and geographic area of Pennsylvania actually voted. Carter exceeded what statistically should have been his vote in Pennsylvania in every category but one— the Catholics. This is the first time that the Catholic grievance really began to show.

Then during the summer, between the two conventions, we did a national poll based on candidate perceptions and issues. We could not find one issue that was statistically significant in predicting the presidential vote of any large group of voters; it was almost entirely a candidate perception election. Almost all of the variants which would account for why people were voting either for Carter or Ford had to do with personal elements and their personal perception, not with issues. When people considered Carter and Ford as individuals, they scaled them on two dimensions. One was a fairly traditional partisan dimension—strong Democrat to strong Republican, economic liberal to economic conservative—the very traditional kind of image. The second was a dimension that we ultimately named "traditional American values," which had to do with all the social issues. We used a number of questions—marijuana, abortion, pornography—to scale social conservatism or liberalism; and in the course of this, we found that foreign policy issues and national defense fell right on that same dimension, in that a strong national defense was seen as a traditional American value and was the same as social conservatism. On our map of voters' perceptions, Governor Carter was way off in one corner, but in the same quadrant with the majority of voters. Essentially, he was seen as an economic liberal and a social conservative—uniquely so.

When we drew a bissector between Ford and Carter on our map, and plotted all the respondents in our poll, we decided that there were three ways that we could win. We were far behind at the time, and there were a lot of dots on Carter's side. One way to win was to change the voters' attitudes and perceptions on issues and policies, which was not a practical thing to consider doing over a ten or twelve week period. The second thing we could do was to nominate the president as a Democrat. And the third thing we could do was to change the perception of Governor Carter as well as that of President Ford. We decided that there was no place on the Republican side of that map where we could theoretically plot Ford and win the election unless we could change the perception of Carter. If Carter stayed where he was, there was no possible way that we could win; we had to move him further than we had to move the president. One of our people asked, "What do we have to do to Carter to move him far enough so that we can win?" The answer was, "The more you make him look like Hubert Humphrey, the better off we are." The Mondale selection did help us begin to move Carter down with the traditional Democrats on the map. The selection obviously helped Carter in other ways, but it was the first thing that began to move him out of the unique position he was in.

The perception of Ford was close to the middle, just slightly to the conservative side of the middle line on "traditional American values." He was perceived as substantially more liberal than Carter on the scale of "traditional American values." When you looked at the difference between Carter and the other Democrats on the economic issues, there was very little. When you looked at the difference between Carter and the other Democrats on the social issues, there was a great deal. When you looked at the difference between Ford and Carter on the economic issues, it was about what you'd expect—the traditional party difference. But when you looked at them on the social issues, the difference was great, and Carter was seen as more conservative. It would be a very hard thing to prove statistically, but it seemed to us that the greatest single factor in putting the president where he was on the social issues scale was his selection of Rockefeller as vice president.

So we tried to decide how we could best move both the president and Carter. Perceptions about both of them were very thin; neither one of them was well known. There were tremendous numbers of people who had no hard view of either of them. The president was perceived positively as a very honest, decent family man, someone who was absolutely sincere in trying to do what he thought was best for the country whether people agreed with him or not. The one big question, and this was not a negative, was simply whether he was smart enough to be president. And then there was a negative perception that he was not a decisive, strong leader—which the Reagan people had already found out. Among people who supported Governor Carter, there were three positive perceptions: one, he was seen as an honest, religious, Christian, moral man who would bring those qualities to government; second, he was seen by almost all Democrats as an acceptable Democrat—there were almost no Democrats who felt he was too far out one way or the other for them; and third, he was seen as conservative in terms of the traditional American values. There were two major questions about him—not necessarily negative. First, and more important, was he qualified to be president, or was he a quick-packaged commodity that had come on the scene very abruptly? Secondly, some people appeared to have some reservations about his religion, and asked whether it might be a little bizarre to be as religious as he was. Beyond these two questions, there were three negatives, three things that we decided had to be the areas of attack. For one thing, he was not seen as a man with any record of accomplishment to qualify him to be president; though some people knew he had been governor of Georgia, they had absolutely no idea of what he had done there. For another thing, he was seen as someone who had not been specific enough on the issues for people to make up their minds to vote for him; this developed into the fuzziness question. And third, he was seen as too inexperienced, particularly if you questioned him in the area of foreign affairs. As we looked to the Kansas City convention in August, these were the areas on which we were basing our plans for the fall campaign.

Two weeks before the Kansas City convention, we had a meeting at Camp David in which we discussed the vice presidential choices and the acceptance speech. We agreed that the acceptance speech ought to talk about the president's general vision of the campaign and the country, and not deal with specific issues or his record in any great detail. The draft of the acceptance speech that we looked at then didn't resemble very much the speech that was finally given, since the president worked on the speech himself a great deal over the next week and during the early part of the week in Kansas City. We had discussed the debate idea, but the decision to insert a paragraph about it was not made until the day of the speech in Kansas City, late in the afternoon. Throughout the summer, it had been my strong feeling that Governor Carter would challenge the president to debate immediately following our convention; and I thought we should be perceived to be the first to challenge.

DUVAL: The Ford campaign needed something dramatic. Our information suggested that, for all practical purposes, the race might be over by the end of September. We did not have a general campaign organization, and we were prohibited by law from spending money until after the nomination, so we were in no position to start implementing our campaign in the month of September. I felt that Governor Carter's campaign would undoubtedly advertise in the month of September and thus be able to solidify his support enough so that he could minimize the likely erosion of his twenty-five point lead and still win by at least eight to ten points. If this was the case, we needed to figure out how to discount everything the governor did during the month of September. We needed something that would cause the country to reserve its judgment. The debates seemed to be the answer. We also had to deal with the competency issue in a dramatic way, and the debates seemed to be a logical way to go on this. The debates might also keep the press from eating us alive on the Rose Garden strategy. I felt that the public would never take seriously the press criticism of the Rose Garden strategy as long as the debates were going on. In addition to these other points, I felt there was virtually no downside risk in the debates. Although some said that the debates would give Governor Carter credibility, the fact of the matter was that he was so far ahead of us in the summer period that that wasn't important. If we could give a general impression of our competency and get the country to reserve its judgment, then the debates would be well worth doing.

TEETER: There's another important point: the president wanted to debate. With all our strategic considerations, if we had decided at some juncture not to go near the debates, I'm not sure that we would have prevailed.

DEVELOPMENT OF FORD CAMPAIGN

The week spent at Vail [Colorado] right after the convention was key to the development of the fall campaign. Everybody knew going into that week that there had to be changes in the campaign organization itself. We had been through a few different campaign chairmen and managers, and had stumbled through the primaries successfully, but now there had to be some changes. We came out of the Vail meeting with a small group of men who got along, who knew and understood each other, who had a strategy in mind for the campaign. Mike Duval took on the debate project; and Jim Baker [third President Ford Committee chairman], Dick Cheney, Stu Spencer [Ford's political director], John Deardourff, and I were five people who got along as one unit and had a strategy in mind for what we were going to try to accomplish in the campaign. Until the last couple of weeks of the campaign, we wanted to send the president out only two or three times and have the advertising carry a very large share of our message. Most importantly, we had a changed candidate. While he never had a good feel for running in the primaries, he now had a pretty high level of confidence. The convention had gone well, his acceptance speech had gone well, and he had a full head of steam; and after spending four or five days going over strategy in Vail, he came away with a very strong personal feeling of who he was in this campaign and who Carter was, and just what it was that we were trying to accomplish. That singularly was the biggest difference between the campaign before and after the convention.

The first memo that we had put together to take to Kansas City outlined the most logical way to get to 270 electoral votes. We had to carry all the states we [Republicans traditionally have] carried, plus Ohio and Wisconsin, plus maybe Maryland, Pennsylvania, and Louisiana. In addition, I felt that we ought not to write off Texas, Florida, New York, and Missouri, where we weren't way behind, because it was very dangerous to get into the situation of not being able to make one mistake on a state. Coming out of the convention and out of Vail, I felt that there was some risk, though not necessarily a probability, that with about two more fumbles, the Ford campaign could lock itself into a McGovern situation [in the 1972 race]. It was very important for us to get very quickly back into the campaign, and I thought the odds were strong that we would. The one thing that we couldn't tolerate was a couple of blunders at that point.

OTTEN: What role did President Ford play in the development of the campaign strategy?

TEETER: President Ford delegated a lot of authority and review; once he agreed on the general nature of the campaign plan, I don't think he got into it very deeply. Any organization is essentially a reflection of the strengths and weaknesses of the man in power. I don't think a candidate has to be involved in the day-to-day decisions in order for a campaign organization to be a very direct reflection of him and the way he runs things. In the general election, President Ford thought he had the right people; and when they agreed on something, he agreed with them. In the primaries, I don't think that President Ford had a very good feel of just what his problems were and what he ought to be doing; and his campaign organization reflected that weakness on his part.

JOHN D. DEARDOURFF (media consultant for Ford): The remarkable thing to me personally was the ease with which President Ford accepted people he did not know very well and could make a judgment quickly on whether their advice was worth hearing. This was why it all came together in a matter of days at Vail. On the other hand, the president was not ever comfortable with bold strokes and resisted them throughout the campaign.

CARTER'S STRATEGY

RANDOLPH: How about the Carter strategy at this point?

HAMILTON JORDAN (campaign manager for Carter): I am interested in Bob Teeter's analysis of which states Ford had to carry to win, because it matches pretty closely our analysis of the electoral vote. We projected that if we carried the Southern states, plus Virginia, Maryland, Missouri, Florida, and Texas, plus Massachusetts, Minnesota, and the District of Columbia, that would bring us to 199 electoral votes. I knew we were going to lose some in there, and we ended up losing Virginia, but we did carry the rest of them. Our base strategy all along was to get the 200 votes, and then get to 270 through one of a variety of ways. If we carried New York and California, that would do it; if we carried New York, Pennsylvania, and Ohio, that would do it. The options were numerous for us, but not for President Ford; he had to carry almost everything he was after, as Bob Teeter said.

In terms of a general comment about the election: I don't think we should have won by over ten points, but I do think we should have won by five or six. Ford ran a much better campaign than I expected him to run, and we ran a much poorer campaign than we should have. One problem was that the national surveys were taken and presented to the public at the time when we were strongest— right after the Democratic convention [in mid-July], where Carter was seen as the leader of a unified, majority party—and at the time when Ford, an incumbent president, was scraping to win the nomination of his own party, during the lowest point of his political campaign. So all of the things that happened to us in the fall were seen in the framework of Carter's slippage; all the news stories were couched in terms of Carter's having blown his lead, and that was a problem almost impossible to handle.

Going into the fall campaign, people liked Jimmy Carter and they liked Gerald Ford. Maybe they liked Ford a little more and liked Carter a little less, but in the final analysis, the perception of Carter as a stronger and more decisive man was probably critical. Carter was seen as not owing anybody anything for his political progress, and this appealed to the electorate. He was different from other politicians, he was strong and decisive, he was not from Washington, he was honest and moral, he was within the mainstream of the Democratic party. On the negative side, he was perceived as being fuzzy. I think that oftentimes voters described Carter as fuzzy when they were unable to verbalize what they really meant. I often felt that people who didn't like him because he was a Southerner said they didn't like him because he was fuzzy. The fuzzy thing really surfaced when Udall began using it effectively [in the primaries], and it was spotted as a vulnerability of Carter's that could be exploited by other candidates. Also on the negative side, we suffered from the weirdo factor. Here was a guy from a different part of the country who talked quite openly about his religion, who had never served in national office before. Historically, the Democratic party has been two pieces—one piece has been Northern and Catholic and urban, and the other part has been Southern and Protestant and rural. Carter was from the part of the Democratic party that did not normally elect the president, but just supported the president. I think President Ford raised the question quite effectively about Carter being a risky candidate. On the other hand, Ford was being perceived as an honest man replacing a dishonest man, as a likable, safe choice who wouldn't rock the boat. But we had a number of issues going against him, particularly economic issues; and the Watergate pardon was always there, particularly with blue collar workers. Another thing that worked against him was that this country had had eight years of

Republican leadership, and it was time for a change. Ford went into the fall campaign with the image of being a bumbler and a man who was not very smart, but I think through the debates and through the campaign, he largely overcame that perception problem. He was viewed throughout the campaign, though, as not as strong a leader as Carter.

I thought the debates were high risk for Ford and very little risk for us. I thought they would confirm what people already thought of Gerald Ford. I thought that the variable in them was Jimmy Carter. It was an opportunity for us to deal with a lot of perception problems that we had. I was surprised that Carter did not do well in the first debate, because he was nervous, and I was surprised that Ford made his mistake in the second debate.* In my opinion, the second debate hurt Ford more than the first hurt us, and through the debates, people learned more about Carter. I think you could make an argument that the debates were decisive in the election. We started out in August after the Republican convention about ten or twelve points ahead, about 52 percent to 41 percent. Although there were news stories that Carter was slipping and Ford was gaining, in fact we weren't slipping, but Ford was gaining undecided voters and gradually edging up on us. We won by two or three points, and if we had not made mistakes, we would have won by five or six. But it was never in the books for us to win by ten or twelve points. Having been through this election, I understand much better the 1948 Truman victory. There are a lot of people who think that when they vote for the president, they are voting for America; and that to vote against the president is to vote against the country. That's very difficult to combat. I think Ford used his incumbency very effectively. He used the presidency much more effectively than I thought he would.

DUVAL: I went back and read [presidential special counsel] Clark Clifford's forty page memo to President Truman in 1947, and I concluded that the biggest mistake that President Ford could make was to have any illusions that he was in a Trumanlike situation. There were no similarities between the 1948 election and 1976. For one thing, in 1948 the incumbent Democrats were a 56 percent majority party; in 1976 you all know what the incumbent Republicans were. For another thing, there was equal financing for the first time this year, and a whole new set of ground rules. Thirdly, in 1948 President

---

*During the second television debate, President Ford defended his signing of the 1975 Helsinki agreement, guaranteeing human rights in Europe. His insistence in the course of this defense that "there is no Soviet domination of Eastern Europe" raised immediate controversy.

Truman had about a 55 percent approval rating, compared to ours. And finally, in 1976 there was an unelected president, with the Watergate pardon and the recession. If Harry Truman had run a Truman campaign in 1976, he would have gotten clobbered, because his speeches were some of the worst speeches I've ever seen. One of the things that made it possible for Truman to win was that most people didn't read him constantly in the newspapers, because the newspapers got tired of reporting him; and people only saw him when they were actually where he was, not on television. There was a strong feeling in our camp, particularly in June and July, that Ford should go out and run a Truman train ride. I had nightmares about his going out there.

JORDAN: I was not drawing an analogy between 1976 and 1948 in terms of the campaigns. It's just that having been through this campaign and having felt the effective use of the president's power, I wonder if Truman was elected not because of the whistlestops, but because he was president of the country. It seems to me that Truman won in 1948 because he was president, and Ford almost won in 1976 because he was president.

OTTEN: How deeply was Mr. Carter involved in developing the general election strategy for his campaign?

PATRICK H. CADDELL (pollster for Carter): The people around Carter were very close to him personally, and he granted responsibility in fairly large blocks. He was always the ultimate arbiter of the positions he took and [of] the campaign in a general way. Though he worked closely with everyone, he really had confidence in his staff and let them make the tactical decisions and some of the strategic ones. He was involved more at the strategic level and less at the tactical level. Unlike some candidates, he didn't interfere in tactical decisions and concentrated on being a good candidate. That was very important throughout the whole campaign, but particularly so in those very hectic primaries.

RANDOLPH: What perceptions of the candidate did the Carter campaign stress in the general election?

GERALD RAFSHOON (media director for Carter): Our data showed that people considered Jimmy more competent than Ford, and we had developed a pretty effective media packaging of his competence and his character, stressing the old values, leadership, and change. In the early part of the campaign, we had found that when we started advertising before our opposition, we could survive the anti-Carter advertising. So we decided to advertise immediately after the Republican convention, and we didn't lose much of the base we had developed. There was a lot of talk that we spent our money early and were out of money when the big Ford pitch started later; but in fact, we spent a total of $260,000 before September 21 and had a really adequate $3 million for the next ten days. Part of our strategy was always to protect our Southern base, so in addition to our national advertising in the South, we did certain things to appeal to Southern chauvinism, saying that we could have a president from the South. And although we didn't talk about them a lot, we used spots that discussed what Governor Reagan had said about President Ford.

SOUTHERN VOTE

NAUGHTON: There was a point when the Ford people seemed to think they had a shot at some of the South—Mississippi, Louisiana. What was that based on? Was Ford simply trying to get Carter to divert more resources there?

NORMAN E. WATTS, JR. (deputy political director for Ford): First of all, the Ford campaign had survey information that Robert Teeter provided. We also had a Southern regional coordinator who knew the South pretty well, and he thought we could make some impression there. We also thought we should keep Governor Carter busy in his own home base in the same way that he kept us busy in states like Illinois and Michigan.

DEARDOURFF: It seemed to me that Ford did pick up considerably at one period, and then something Carter did worked very well—probably the appeal to Southern pride. At the right moment in the campaign, in the last week or so, the Carter people came on with very effective regional advertising aimed exclusively at Southern voters that persuaded people to stay with their man.

JORDAN: In March and April in the primaries, it had been an enormously strong factor in the South that a guy from the South might actually be nominated by the party, might actually be president. By the fall, the novelty of this Southern thing had worn off a bit, but we [Carter people] planned to stir it up again toward the end of the campaign. I believe Carter got a disproportionate number of the undecided voters in Southern states because he was a Southerner.

RAFSHOON: Plus our black media started in the South.

JORDAN: The turnout in the black areas in the South was fantastic; in some of the precincts, Carter was getting 93 or 95 percent of the black votes.

WATTS: It was our information in the Ford campaign that Carter was having to pull back media buys and the like in other places in order to concentrate in the South.

JORDAN: We did some radio stuff in the South in late October that we hadn't planned to, and we did have an increased commitment in the South, but we weren't taking media money away from other places.

RAFSHOON: We never reduced our media elsewhere. The money for media in the South came from other sources in the campaign, such as field organization.

JORDAN: From the beginning, we did not want it to be said that we were taking the South for granted. So in the month of September, on the way to whereever we were going—Northeast, West, or Midwest—Carter would always stop and do Southern states. Then toward the end of the campaign, we did the same thing. I always felt that we could carry every Southern state. We were a little concerned about Mississippi, but Carter went there and things settled down. We were a lot concerned about Louisiana; that's the only Southern state I thought President Ford had a chance of carrying, and so we made a decision to send the governor in there.

TEETER: Louisiana is 37 percent Catholic, and the one Southern state I thought Ford might pick off. We [Ford people] kept poking around and looking for something that would allow us a little flexibility in our electoral strategy. If it worked out right, our electoral strategy would give us 276 votes if we carried Ohio and Wisconsin. One mistake and we would be under—and we made two mistakes. We kept looking at Virginia and Missouri as possibilities for us.

CARTER CAMPAIGN ORGANIZATION

JAMES M. PERRY (columnist, *National Observer*): Right after the Democratic convention, there seemed to be an immense pause; the Carter campaign just seemed to sit. It must have been doing things, but there seemed to be a very long delay in getting going.

JORDAN: Carter was in Plains most of the time with an occasional trip out, but we were busting our ass to put the fall campaign together. Tim Kraft and Phil Wise assembled a first rate field organization, and we got control of our budget. Rafshoon was working on the media, and Pat Caddell started doing surveys in critical states. The time was spent well.

BENJAMIN D. BROWN (deputy campaign director for Carter): There were some things that had to be done in order for Carter to avoid the mistakes of 1972. McGovern had won a brilliant primary victory, but the McGovern people were never able to work it out with the party structure. Our field people were working to solidify the relationship between our primary forces and our state party people, which was a problem in many states. In order to get a maximum vote, we had to sit down with the constituent groups of the party, particularly the black community. We really had some problems in the primary, for instance, in Ohio, in the twenty-first district. We had to make people like [Ohio Congressman] Lou Stokes and others believe that we were real about what we were doing, and that they would be a part of a Democratic victory. Although we came out of the New York convention [in mid-July] with an aura of unity, there was still a lot of internal work that had to be done between the Carter people and the party structure people. I think we did that work successfully to some extent, but it wasn't completed, and we'll have to keep at it for the next four years.

DAVID S. BRODER (associate editor, *Washington Post*): What is the evidence that the Carter campaign achieved anything in terms of its relationship with Democratic party organizations or groups that were not part of the original Carter coalition?

JORDAN: Carter was an outsider who had rapidly captured the party nomination, so there was a need for him to establish relationships with elements of the party that he had not known before, like labor. Carter developed a relationship with the AFL–CIO which finally resulted in its enthusiastic support in the last three or four weeks of the campaign. But we paid a price with the independent voters: Carter was a guy who wasn't supposed to owe anybody anything, but he kept going to see George Meany [president of AFL–CIO], just like politicians have always done. Sometimes the things we had to do over the summer to bring together the elements of the Democratic party helped us with Democrats but hurt us with independent voters. From state to state, we had party chairpersons and governors and senators that helped us, sat on their hands, or, in a few cases, were against us.

JOSEPH L. POWELL, JR. (press secretary for Carter): The primary campaigns in the states were coordinated by about four people, and we just rolled them over and over. But you can't do that in a general election, so we had to get things organized locally. In 1975 we had recognized that we weren't going to get any national publicity, and we went ahead to get it locally. In the fall of 1976, our problem was that we got too much national publicity, and there wasn't anything we could do about that either. There was no way on God's earth we could shake the fuzziness question in the general election, no matter what Carter did or said. He could have spent the whole campaign doing nothing but reading substantive speeches from morning to night and still have had that image in the national press. I felt that we had to try to reinvigorate and use the local coverage. In about fifteen or sixteen states, we established local press operations that reported back to the national headquarters and also worked with the state coordinators. It took time to put these local operations into place. In 1975 we would have been dead without the coverage we got from local television stations and local newspapers; and that was true in 1976 as well.

OTTEN: While the Carter people were putting their organization in place, why wasn't Carter himself moving around the country more?

POWELL: First, I thought he was overexposed. And second, the type of publicity we were getting was the best we had gotten during the whole campaign period, certainly better than we would have gotten out on the road. If we could have stayed in Plains until October, as Ford stayed in the White House until October, we would have won by five or ten points.

JORDAN: In my opinion, one of the reasons that we had problems during the primaries in May was that we were overexposed. Carter was a media phenomenon, and people were tired of hearing about "Jimmy Carter this" and "Jimmy Carter that." So I felt that our best posture during the summer, and certainly after the Democratic convention, was to lie low in Plains. We never considered going on the road.

LYN NOFZIGER (campaign consultant for Reagan and Dole): Was any effort made to bring in the leadership of the other Democratic candidates during this period? Did Carter's campaign organization include people from Udall, Bayh, and so forth?

JORDAN: Early on, we had three very talented people that we just rotated in the primary period from Iowa to Massachusetts to Pennsylvania to Ohio to Florida to Wisconsin to Maryland and then to New Jersey. Of the forty-five or fifty state coordinators in the general election, only five or six had been involved in our campaign previously. Paul Sullivan, for instance, who did a superb job for us in Illinois, had worked in Udall's campaign back in New York and Wisconsin. Terry O'Connell had run Jackson's campaign in New York and California. Dan Horgan had actually whipped us in the New Jersey primary, and he ended up running our Ohio campaign. So we had a lot of talent from other campaigns that we sent into states as coordinators.

REAGAN-FORD RELATIONSHIP

NAUGHTON: There was a lot of discussion about whether or not the Reagan and Ford forces got together after the convention and worked in harmony successfully.

NOFZIGER: When President Ford went to Vail after the convention, none of the Reagan people was invited—not Governor Reagan, or John Sears, or [Nevada Senator] Paul Laxalt [chairman of Citizens for Reagan]. There was no effort to unify the campaign structure at that point, though later on some of us [from the Reagan campaign] got involved. People asked where Reagan was in all this. Two weeks after the August convention, Paul Laxalt called a meeting of people from the Republican National Committee, the congressional committee, and the Senate committee to see how they could utilize Reagan, but nobody contacted Reagan to ask him to do anything. It was two weeks before President Ford finally called Reagan and asked him if he would help. Reagan suggested Dick Cheney get together with Mike Deaver, who was Reagan's chief of staff, so they could work out a schedule. Almost two weeks more, and nothing had been done. I spoke to Stu Spencer about it, and Stu talked to Deaver, who had been waiting for Cheney's call. So it was a long time before the organization actually sat down to try to work out Reagan's participation in the campaign.

WATTS: I think most of this chronology is accurate, but I don't remember any phone calls from Governor Reagan asking, "What can

I do?" About six weeks before the election, the Ford people did pro-
pose a schedule to the governor; but even though there was communication back and forth, we never received an answer on numbers of
days or appearances or just what he'd do to participate.

DAVID A. KEENE (Southern coordinator for Reagan): People felt
the need to come out of the convention with something resembling a
united party, and in most of the states, the Reagan people and the
Ford people did get together. In many cases, they co-chaired the
general election campaign and worked together, sometimes with
success and sometimes without success in terms of the outcome. At
the state level, as opposed to what may or may not have happened in
Washington, there was a good deal of cooperation.

WATTS: Ford wouldn't have carried California without the Reagan
people—no question about that. The governor himself sent telegrams
and made phone calls. But we didn't get it together in the national
campaign, and I understand that the governor's schedule got pretty
crowded.

DUVAL: In terms of our dealings with Governor Reagan, the Ford
campaign just screwed up. But in a larger sense, we were successful in
creating a perception of the president's winnability, and that resulted
in a fairly unified party.

OTTEN: Would it have made any difference if Reagan had been involved earlier and more actively?

NOFZIGER: I don't think that Reagan could have swung another
200,000 votes in Texas, but he did speak for Ford in Texas and a
number of other places and did a half hour television show. He carried California for the president.

VOTERS' PERCEPTIONS OF CANDIDATES

DUVAL: What's important is not the specific act—like Reagan's
going in—but the dynamics of a situation. It's the reaction to an
event and the next reaction to that reaction that you've got to think
through all the way. If Ford had gone into a different state and had
thus provoked a reaction on the part of Governor Carter's campaign,
things might have been changed around. For another example, once
the charge of fuzziness got rolling, there was nothing the Carter peo-

ple could do about it. The question was whether we [Ford people] should go with the fuzziness charge first or with the charge that Carter was not being specific. That was an important tactical decision. It's obvious that a lot of people thought that the governor's position was their position on a given issue, when often it wasn't. The Ford campaign could have led with an attack which said, "What is his position?" and tried, for example on the abortion question, to make him spell out what his position was. That might have led Carter to react by trying to fuzz that issue, which Ford could have then capitalized on.

POWELL: Because people kept saying that no one knew who Carter was, there were repeated and painful attempts by us to explain who this man really was, sometimes to the point of absolute absurdity. That's why we [Carter people] thought he was overexposed at times. Actually, people didn't know anything about Gerald Ford either, but there's a natural assumption that if a guy is president, people know him and you don't need to explain.

CADDELL: Given what had happened in Viet Nam and Watergate, Carter as an unknown had a real plus in the beginning. In the season of conventions, he was what everyone wanted without anyone's having to make any commitment to a decision. In June, Carter was about fifteen points ahead in some of the public surveys, but almost half of the people could not answer most of the questions about him, and close to a full third had problems answering any of them. At that point, he had the most difficult problem a presidential candidate can experience, which was people's doubt about his being qualified to be president—particularly when it came to foreign policy. He was perceived as someone who was either fuzzy or nonspecific, if you want to split that hair. He was perceived as a strong person, stronger than Ford, but people were uneasy with him as a person. When we [Carter people] went looking for our natural constituency groups—people who were normally Democrats but had moved toward being independents with Democratic tendencies—we had serious problems with young voters, Catholics, and women. On the other hand, we were doing very well in rural areas, and with Protestants. The Democratic convention served a very important purpose in giving Carter exposure, particularly in his acceptance speech. That exposure eliminated some of the problems he had and deferred others. The competence question disappeared forever, though the experience question reappeared in a milder form. The sense of Carter as a visionary remained high from that point on, as did the sense that he could take charge; and the level of people's general uneasiness with him declined significantly.

We did some surveys after the convention until the general election and took people through a series of open-ended questions. We asked about Carter on social issues, and got a tremendous plus; he was perceived as being really in line with most people's thinking. However, when we asked people to think about Carter as president, it was clear that some people in the interview began to have doubts and some actually decided not to vote for him at the end of the interview. It was clear that this doubt would generally show up later.

The surveys right after the convention reflected the buildup of expectations—we were still holding a quarter of the Republicans, a third of the Reagan voters, and over half the conservatives—but then our drop started immediately after the convention stopped. Over that weekend, the Harris poll gave us a thirty-nine point lead; we were down to thirty-three by the time the Gallup poll came out; and by the Republican convention we were sliding much quicker. We could see every day that the thing was beginning to shape itself into the beginning of a normal general election. Large segments of the public were simply not going to take an unknown and make him president. Carter was seen as a risk, whereas Ford was safe. William Loeb [of the Manchester *Union Leader*] put it in more pejorative terms the day after election with the headline, "Shifty Beats Stupid."

Ford was unnaturally low for a while: in the Gallup poll, he had a lower percentage than George McGovern ever had in the public polls in 1972, and he suffered from a job rating that was sometimes fourteen or twenty points below his personal rating as an individual. He also suffered from the perception that he was not a strong leader; and even toward the end of the campaign, people would mention the Nixon pardon. Although the economic issues were not cutting as hard as some of us expected, Ford did get some blame on the economy. Carter, on the other hand, was perceived as someone who was concerned, who would take charge of the government, who was probably able to be a decisive leader. The problem was that people weren't sure what he would lead toward—he was still perceived as fuzzy. Many of the perceptions that people had had in the July period were changed as he dealt with issues, and as some people discovered that he really was a Democrat. Early on, the Carter people agreed to ignore that lead factor in July and to try to solidify our Democratic base. We needed to increase the depth of commitment among voters who were traditionally Democrats. As it turned out in the election, our ability to hold rural voters and Protestants really made the difference.

FORD MEDIA CAMPAIGN

OTTEN: How did the Ford campaign, and in particular the Ford media campaign, attempt to capitalize on the strengths and weaknesses of each of the two candidates?

DEARDOURFF: The Ford advertising effort in the general election began at the time of the Republican convention. I had not been involved prior to the convention, and in fact, I had never met president Ford until the convention was over. I remember meeting with Gerry Rafshoon several weeks thereafter, and hearing Gerry say that while he wasn't sure he was the world's best advertiser, he was certain he was the world's foremost expert on Jimmy Carter; I thought to myself what a tremendous advantage that could be, to really know your candidate. I had a different problem, or maybe a different opportunity in a way: I started with some serious reservations about being involved at all; I did not know the president; I had not had access to any of the planning documents at any stage; and at the time of the convention, while everybody else was worried about getting the nomination, I was holed up in a house in Kansas City with my partner Doug Bailey and [advertising consultant] Malcolm MacDougall, trying to produce an advertising plan for the general election. We had Bob Teeter's research, and we spoke from time to time during that week with people in the Ford campaign. But it was essentially without any other inputs that we were trying to produce a document that could be presented to the president immediately after the convention at Vail for his approval or otherwise.

We also had to use part of that week for production purposes. We wanted footage of the president's family actively participating on his behalf at the convention, and we wanted film of the convention itself, particularly of the president's acceptance speech. We also filmed short interviews with about 120 convention delegates from various parts of the country about why they were supporting President Ford, and these were later intermixed with some people talking about why they did not care much for Jimmy Carter. We were producing at the same time that we were trying to think about what we wanted to produce, but we didn't have much choice because the time was so limited.

We had gotten to the point in the campaign where the public had to choose between two men who were addressing themselves to questions about the condition of the country today and what should be done about the problems the country will have in the future. It was an argument between two individuals who were arguing about a very narrow range of things. It was our feeling that we had to sustain the argument that the country, while it was not over its problems, was much better off than it had been two and a half years before on a variety of scales, and that the president's direction for the future was preferable to the uncertainty of what the Carter direction was. This was essentially a candidate perception election, and though the issues played a part in the campaign in that they reinforced underlying perceptions of the candidates, they were not terribly important standing alone.

On the Ford side, it was clearly a major negative that he was way behind, whether it was by fifteen points or thirty points or whatever. He was a Republican, and that is a serious disadvantage to any candidate running almost anywhere today. He was a Republican who had been appointed by the least popular president in America's history, and who had then pardoned that president in advance of any indictment or trial. Unemployment was high, inflation was going down but was still unacceptably high, and we could not find many issues in August that seemed to cut in any way that was helpful to us. We decided that there were five things that we wanted to accomplish with the advertising campaign: first of all, we wanted to strengthen the personal dimension of the president; second, we wanted to strengthen what we called his leadership dimension; third, we wanted to present the Ford record in some convincing way if we could; fourth, we wanted to try to indicate that the president had some program for the future of the country; and fifth, crucially important, we needed to raise serious questions about Jimmy Carter. We could go part way with a positive presentation of the president's strengths, but we could not win unless we could change substantially the impression that then existed about Carter, both in terms of his position on some kind of ideological scale and in terms of the perception of him as a human being. I thought we had to raise the positive impression of the president before we could risk going at Carter heavily, and that the timing of that so-called "negative advertising" had to be just right. In retrospect, I think we may have missed by several days in terms of the timing. I have a feeling now that if the campaign had ended on Sunday [October 31] rather than on Tuesday [November 2], we might have won.

We claimed at the time that we had a strategy that involved delaying our advertising until after the first debate [September 23]. This was a practical matter, since we had no advertising. In order to fill the vacuum a little bit, we ran an edited version of the president's acceptance speech on network television. This bought us a little time, but, lacking the excitement of the actual convention to back it up, it did not have a tremendous impact or a very big audience. The first commercials that we made were all designed to elaborate on and try to improve the perception of the president himself: we did a five minute biographical film, a five minute film involving the Ford family, and a five minute film called "Leadership," which was an attempt to describe the difference between the way in which President Ford operated in the White House and the way in which President Nixon had operated. It was our feeling all along that we had to try to drive as deep a wedge as we could in the public perception between Ford and Nixon. Then we also tried to present President Ford's accomplishments during two and a half years, using five minute films. And we had a special five minute film on agriculture that was used only in the rural markets in the country.

The personal impressions of the president that we were trying to strengthen were those that related first of all to his basic intelligence, since there was a question in the public's mind about this. Through the biographical film, we tried to demonstrate that at every stage of his life he had been a success because of a combination of basic intellectual capacity and a propensity to work very hard. The film showed the president as an Eagle Scout, an honor student, captain of the football team, a successful student at Yale Law School competing with an outstanding class of his peers, and then in the military. The treatment of both the football and the military record was obviously designed to speak to the question of social conservatism— the traditional American values. That biographical film served a very useful purpose.

The five minute film on the Ford family ran principally on daytime television. We felt that this was an attractive family and that the family ethic in America is still a very strong one; these were extraordinarily attractive human beings in their own right, and their interrelationship was an important thing to project. We also did a five minute film in which we attempted to demonstrate that the president had a style of leadership different from his predecessors; and though this might lead to longer periods of time before decisions were made, the end result was not one of indecision or bad decisions. We tried to get at the question of President Ford's accomplishments by re-creating what it was like in 1974 when he became president. On some absolute scale, the accomplishments might not be overly impressive; but if you measured them in terms of the whole Watergate mentality in August 1974, there was a sense that things were in fact substantially better and that people felt better about things. The song "I'm Feeling Good About America" was an obvious attempt to create a good feeling about the country, and to give the president a certain amount of credit for having improved the situation.

During the whole campaign, we asked, "Are things as bad as Jimmy Carter says they are, or are they getting better, and is it worth the risk of accepting Carter, about whom you know very little, as opposed to a man who seems to be solid and stable?" We felt from the very beginning that we had to go after Carter, and we did it that way. Immediately after the first debate, we sent a camera crew to six different cities and just walked up and down the streets asking people whom they intended to vote for. If they said they were for Ford, we asked them what they didn't like about Jimmy Carter. We used their totally spontaneous remarks, obviously later edited to length. We were attempting through the voices of ordinary people to get at the negatives that were coming out of our polling about Carter—the fact that his record as governor of Georgia had been nothing extraordinary, that he was, as people said repeatedly, "wishy-washy." If one commercial ever stuck, it was the one in which three people in a row repeatedly suggested that Carter was wishy-washy; I think it got at a true feeling about the man. We also had a commercial that began with part of a Carter commercial that said, "What he did for Georgia, he'll do for America." We showed that, and then we showed some specifics on what he had done for Georgia. The anti-Carter commercials went on the air about mid-October.

OTTEN: Were there any commercials aimed specifically at Catholic ethnic voters?

DEARDOURFF: We did one series of commercials showing the president with various groups of people—farmers, factory workers, young people, senior citizens—talking about things like taxes, crime, housing, and other problems that the upper end blue collar worker would have. We ran those in the major industrial states pretty heavily.

MARK A. SIEGEL (executive director, Democratic National Committee): Ford's media was very "white" until the night before the election. Since you're very sensitive to the outreach of the Republican party, why didn't you attempt to make some breakthrough there?

DEARDOURFF: We did use blacks in all of our commercials—factory workers, young kids, old people—but there was no major effort to attract blacks. We did have some black advertising, but the polls showed so little opportunity for us in that area because of the perception of the party that it did not seem worth spending a lot of money.

CARTER MEDIA CAMPAIGN

RAFSHOON: The first part of the Ford media seemed similar to what the Carter campaign had done in the primaries—building on the president's character, his family, and the traditional American values. That was something that Ford needed to do, and it was also something that we [Carter people] needed to do as our primary campaign went national. The first part of our national media campaign went into the fact that Jimmy was more of a competent individual than President Ford, and that people needed to know more about his record as governor. We had an expanded biography similar to the one we used in the primaries, we had a five minute program on his record as governor, and we had a film on Jimmy Carter's vision of America. Our data indicated that we had a lack of perception among some traditional Democratic groups, such as Catholics, in Northern areas like Ohio and New York, so we did some advertising that would position Governor Carter as someone who, while not the most traditional Democrat, still had traditional Democratic coalition ties. In view of the fuzziness problem, we used spots that had Jimmy Carter speaking on the issues—reorganization, the economy, welfare reform, jobs. We used Southern pride advertising in the South, also some ads featuring Ronald Reagan on President Ford. We felt that Ford's negative advertising on Jimmy was very effective, but we also felt that the Ford people might be baiting us to come out and use negative advertising on President Ford, which would not have been a good idea. So we just had Governor Carter talk more about the state of the economy, the lack of leadership in Washington, the need for reorganizing government, the drift, the lack of vision in our government; but he didn't mention President Ford. We did not feel that there was any way to answer their charge that Jimmy was wishy-washy. Our research showed that the Nixon pardon was the one issue that probably would have been effective in a negative spot, but I think that would have backfired. Also, Governor Carter had said he wasn't going to talk about the pardon.

RICHARD MOE (campaign director for Mondale): Mondale raised this question with Carter shortly after the convention, and they just simply agreed that this was going to be one of the things they disagreed on. Mondale felt very strongly that the pardon should be raised as a campaign issue, but Governor Carter felt equally strongly that it shouldn't be.

RAFSHOON: Following the debate between Mondale and Dole [October 15], we did a negative spot that we thought was very effective—a Mondale-Dole spot which asked, "Which of these two men do you want a heartbeat away from the presidency?" We started using that just about everyplace, and we put it on the networks a couple of times. We didn't play it so heavily in the South because we were downplaying Mondale in the South.

DEARDOURFF: I believe that paid media advertising in a presidential campaign is effective in direct proportion to the way in which it either reinforces or is forced to fight against what is being reported in the news. I think there is an inverse ratio between the effectiveness of paid advertising and the amount and quality of news coverage. Paid advertising, while very effective, is less effective in a presidential campaign than in almost any other kind of political endeavor. In the Ford campaign, one of our problems was that at a crucial point in the campaign we found our advertising fighting against the perceptions of the president that were being created elsewhere, in the debates.

IMPACT OF DEBATES

OTTEN: Both sides claimed to think that the debates were a plus. Carter said he couldn't have won without them, and they were said to be key to the Ford strategy. Could both sides win?

CADDELL: I didn't accept the premise that the campaign was going to end on Labor Day, because there were just too many factors. And if there continued to be a focus on Governor Carter and his ability to be president, the debates would offer an opportunity to have Jimmy Carter on the same stage as the president, so that judgments could be made about him in comparison with Ford. The debates were an opportunity to remove any growing doubts about Carter, and to devalue to some extent some of the news events that took place. The timing of the debates was very important to Carter. All three debates came at points in the campaign where Carter was in decline in our surveys. The first debate [September 23] helped stop the slide after the *Playboy* interview,* the second debate [October 7] again held up a decline, and the third debate [October 22] did the same.

*Early on in the campaign, candidate Carter gave an interview to *Playboy* magazine, in which he offered his views on religion, morality, and sex. The interview was the center of controversy when it was published in the fall of 1976.

DEARDOURFF: The Ford campaign had no choice except to adopt a very high risk strategy at Vail. We thought the debates would postpone the decisionmaking of undecided voters, as they did, and allow us to get going. On this score, the first debate was seen as particularly crucial to us, because we could create the impression in people's minds that it was almost sinful for them to decide before they'd had a chance to see the two candidates going at each other. Ford was perceived at that point in the polls as less competent, so the debates would be a plus if they improved the president's competence dimension. The first debate clearly did that, and one debate would have been ideal! After the first one, though, it's harder to justify the debates as a positive element in the Ford campaign.

TEETER: We [Ford people] thought that the debates might serve to push Carter into specifics. People tended to think that Governor Carter held the same positions as they did, regardless of what their positions were. We felt that if we could push him to specific positions on a number of issues, he had to lose some people. But after the first one, the debates were a minus. It took us six days to correct the mistake that the president made in the second debate, and that was a very, very important minus in the election. We polled a little bit during those six days, and we saw that we stopped moving up. We had been in a period where the polling data showed we were going up and Carter was coming down; the second debate just flattened that right out and we gained nothing for another twelve or thirteen days. But the polling information was not critical in the president's decision about what to do.

DUVAL: In general, people who saw the debate did not perceive the president's remark about Eastern Europe as a mistake; but in some measure, people perceived that the press had created the impression of a mistake. This perception, coupled with the Carter attack on the president, tended to bring people back to the president.

TEETER: In the polling we did starting in the last minute of the second debate, between 11:00 and 1:00 that night, the question of who did a better job in the debate came out Ford 44 percent, Carter 43. Between 9:00 in the morning and noon the next day, it was Ford 32, Carter 44. Between noon and 5:00 in the afternoon, it was Ford 21, Carter 43. Between 5:00 and midnight the day after, it was Ford 17, Carter 62. Reports of the debate had reemphasized the president as a mistake prone, inept bumbler, exactly what we had spent six or seven weeks trying to get away from.

RANDOLPH: After the Eastern Europe gaffe, it seemed that the Ford people could not control their candidate, and the Carter people could not stop Carter from accusing Ford of being brainwashed.

RAFSHOON: We [Carter people] were slightly gleeful when the president made his mistake, and we were more gleeful when we went to the pressroom and they asked us about it. The significance of the mistake kept setting in more and more the next couple of days. I'm not going to say that Governor Carter went overboard in taking advantage of the mistake, but we were seeing him on television getting a little too shrill about it. This came through clearly on television, but Jimmy and the people around him on the plane didn't perceive it. It took a couple of days to get the word to Jimmy that this was what we were seeing from the press and the television. He slacked off then, but the damage was done.

DEARDOURFF: There were several people discussing decisions with the president, and half of them were on one end of the country and half of them were on the other. The ones who were with the president were spending most of their time being hurtled through space in an aluminum tube called an airplane, and couldn't see what was happening anywhere outside the plane. The fidelity of communication became extremely poor. Some of us back East could not effectively communicate what the real impact of the Eastern Europe thing was. The president did not, I think, believe that the impact was as severe as we thought it was; and as a result, it took a while to get everybody together with him in the same room and say, "Look, the fact is this."

RAFSHOON: One of the biggest problems in a campaign is that the candidate is constantly going before big and partisan crowds. It was a little hard to say to Jimmy, when 40,000 people were out there cheering him as he knocked the president and talked traditional Democratic rhetoric, that he was wrong and we were right because we saw it on television last night. Right after the Eastern Europe thing, we made it a practice to tape the evening news on all three channels every night and send it down to Plains when Jimmy got back at the end of the week to let him look at it, look at how it was being perceived.

RANDOLPH: Why did Carter decide to do the *Playboy* interview?

CADDELL: Other people had done interviews; Jerry Brown had done an interview earlier in the year and it had turned out to be quite positive for him. I don't think that when the interview was done people thought about how it would be perceived when published in late September or the middle of October in an entirely different context. The key thing for an unknown challenger in any presidential campaign is to avoid mistakes that raise questions about his judgment, and the *Playboy* interview raised questions about Carter's judgment. It wasn't the language that he used, but the fact that he did the interview. We happened to be in the middle of a national survey at the time, going right into the first debate, and we saw that the interview had a tremendous impact—we were dropping quite rapidly. Then the first debate fortunately changed the focus. Although very few people would say that the interview changed their vote or had an impact on them, you could see at the time that it did. The judgment problem was rising, and our problems with women were really exacerbated at that point. It's hard to say what effect Ford's negative media was having at the same time.

RAFSHOON: At this point, I felt that we needed to get away from the traditional Democratic rhetoric. Carter was an independent candidate who had in the primaries appealed to conservatives, Republicans, and independents. He was talking now a lot about Roosevelt and Truman and past Democratic policies, and I thought we were beginning to pick up in groups of the old Democratic coalition and so didn't need to promote that any more.

CADDELL: Governor Carter had a difficult time being the candidate that his party wanted him to be. During the primaries, he had a hard time assimilating the traditional Northern Democratic rhetoric, whether it was about the economy or about the party. He spent much of September trying to figure out how to do that and then how to go back to his own themes. Just prior to the second debate, there was a period of several days when he really began to find his stride. He could discuss things in his own context, and make it work. Then we ran right into the second debate, and all his efforts were directed toward dealing with the president's mistake. Then it took him a while again to get back to his own style. He never was a really good speaker to large crowds; he's not a stump speaker. His real effectiveness in the primaries had been in the media coverage of his personal campaigning.

TEETER: It was really hard to absorb the three debates into the general flow of things in the campaign. When the direction got started in the fall campaign, the three debates were just dropped right in the middle and artificially changed the direction of things.

DEARDOURFF: Throughout the Ford campaign, I think we achieved less than satisfactory public perception of presidential leadership. We needed to emphasize four things about the president: integrity, competence, experience, and vision. I think we were on our way with three of those four, but one of the great weaknesses of the campaign was that we never even remotely approached the vision dimension. Whether or not you agreed with his vision of the future, Governor Reagan had a vision that people perceived. On the matter of vision, we kept running up against a wall. I think that [Ford's] twenty-five years as the leader of the [Republican] opposition [in the House of Representatives] had taken its toll.

ROLE OF VICE PRESIDENTIAL CANDIDATES

OTTEN: What was the effect of vice presidential candidate Dole in this area?

TEETER: After the vice presidential debate, I expect that Senator Mondale was a slight plus to Governor Carter; but I think Senator Dole ended up not having any effect on the Ford vote. The debate gave the Carter people an issue to talk about—the comparison between Dole and Mondale.

NOFZIGER: But if you look at the farm state campaign, especially in Washington, eastern Oregon, and the Central Valley of California, I think that you will find that Ford did better in those areas after Dole went through than he had expected to do.

TEETER: It was very clear that when Dole went into rural areas anywhere, he helped Ford. We tested him in given media markets— Indiana, Iowa, eastern Washington—and we concluded that his presence there would help. But the presence of any candidate for vice president, whoever it might be, would have helped. My problem with Dole was what his candidacy suggested about where the party was positioning itself, and about the status quo orientation of the campaign.

CADDELL: As the campaign was wearing on, our [Carter's] data showed that Dole was gaining a greater and greater negative rating;

and going into the vice presidential debate, his positive and negative ratings were not very different. Then coming out of that debate, his negative rating actually surpassed the positive rating. Our studies showed that about 47 percent of the people agreed with the objective statement that Bob Dole wasn't qualified to be president. This helped us particularly with some groups that we thought Carter should be doing better with—younger voters, independents.

NAUGHTON: What relationship developed between the White House and Bob Dole?

NOFZIGER: As far as I know, whenever Bob Dole talked to the president, the president said, "You're doing fine, keep at it." In the Dole part of the race, we had some feeling that we were not getting as much direction as we would have liked; Dole felt as if he had been just turned loose at the beginning while they were putting together the rest of the campaign. There were some concerns in Ford headquarters that Bob might go off the deep end somewhere, but it never came back to us that they felt he actually had. On the other side, I gather that the Mondale people sat down with Carter and that there was a fairly good discussion of what Mondale's role was.

MOE: The Mondale people accepted the invitation from the Carter people to come down to Atlanta and integrate with them. It was quickly agreed that Mondale's role in the campaign would be to reassure the traditional constituencies—labor, minorities, ethnics. Historically, the presidential candidate has been nominated because he's had the support of those constituencies, and then he has picked a vice presidential candidate to reach beyond; but this was the reverse. We spent almost all of our time with the traditional constituencies. We became increasingly convinced that Dole would not want to debate, even though he had challenged us. But we wanted very much to have that debate. Negotiations got strung out almost endlessly.

OTTEN: Why did the Ford people not sit down with the Dole people?

DUVAL: The president of the United States and his running mate were two grown men and experienced politicians; they talked to one another, and they worked it out. I don't know what the president said to Senator Dole—they were alone.

TEETER: Ford and Dole talked periodically through the campaign, and staff people talked regularly. It is part of the president's style, the way he deals with his cabinet and people in the White House, to expect them to go out and do the job they have to do as they see fit.

McCARTHY CANDIDACY

OTTEN: Did the candidacy of Eugene McCarthy affect the Carter campaign?

CADDELL: McCarthy was there, and there was nothing we could do about it. Our expectation was that his vote would decline as the race began—which it did. We did not think that he would gather a large number of votes, but there was always the problem that his votes might make the difference. In our last survey, he was getting about 3 percent, and was going down. Some of his vote was made up of people who had decided not to vote for either Ford or Carter under any circumstances. Part of the rest of his vote was a potential Ford vote, but most of the rest was a potential Carter vote. Overall, about a quarter of it was nonvote, about a quarter of it was the president's vote, and maybe half or a little less than half was the Carter vote.

TEETER: Ford's research showed a little bit more of the vote coming from Carter, but certainly there was at least that quarter or third that was not voting for anybody else. We couldn't find many votes that McCarthy was getting from Ford.

SIEGEL: At some point in the campaign, Patrick Caddell and I were talking about the McCarthy problem, and as matter of concern I started mapping the states where he was and wasn't going to be on the ballot. Without checking with the Carter staff, I took a specific interest in a few states, particularly New York. There were irregularities in New York, and eventually the courts decided that McCarthy's people hadn't complied with the statute. It was a very long and expensive process that the Carter campaign was not directly involved in.

ROBERT J. KEEFE (campaign director for Jackson): One of the successes of the Republican convention was that there was no effective conservative ticket running thereafter. The conservative meeting in Chicago [in late August] failed to put together a Jesse Helms candidacy, which would probably have hurt the Republicans more than McCarthy hurt the Democrats.

TEETER: The effect would not have been so great in this particular election because of the states the Ford campaign had to carry. Obviously Helms would have hurt us because we had such a very small margin, but the fact was that Helms' greatest effect would have been in the South.

IMPORTANCE OF NATIONAL PARTY ORGANIZATIONS

OTTEN: How important a role was the Republican National Committee playing throughout the Ford campaign?

EDDIE MAHE, JR. (executive director, Republican National Committee): The Republican National Committee had three responsibilities that were agreed on between us and both the Ford and Reagan campaign committees before the convention. Following the Ford nomination, we undertook those three responsibilities. We took responsibility for having the $3.2 million available to the party for the general election campaign. We also took responsibility for setting up and implementing the voter identification and voter turnout delivery system. With the convention in late August, there were obvious time constraints in terms of what the campaign would be able to take on, given the time necessary to install six or seven thousand telephones and get the necessary lists put together. We did this job for the entire Republican ticket rather than just for the president, because the very deep problems with a similar effort in 1972 with the Committee to Re-elect the President had created great reservations about participating in this kind of program in a lot of state and local party organizations. Finally, we took the responsibility both for the initial effort made in Carter opposition research, and then for its continuation throughout the campaign. In terms of contribution to the final result, I think that probably our telephone effort made the difference in states that the president carried very narrowly. We were up against an extraordinarily sophisticated and well-financed effort in support of the Democratic nominee; if we had not had some equivalent effort, I think we might well have been eliminated in a few of those states.

OTTEN: How important was the party organization on the Democratic side?

SIEGEL: At the top level, the Democratic party structure and the Carter campaign structure meshed well in terms of personal relationships and operating relationships. There may have been some problems, though, between our people in the field and the Carter field operatives, principally concerning the one major task we [Democratic National Committee] performed for the campaign and for other Democrats as well—the voter registration project. We spent approximately $2 million in that effort, and accomplished registration of approximately three million people in fourteen targeted states. Unlike the Republicans, we did not have a task of voter identification. In general, we know who the unregistered people in this country are, and how they would vote if they were registered. So we went after them, especially blacks, latinos, the poor, and youths. If we did indeed register 3 million people who wouldn't have participated otherwise, and if approximately 2.4 million of those people voted as we think they did, that obviously is very important in terms of the 1.7 million margin in the final vote.

The money question was very difficult for us and generated bad press. We have not yet raised the $3.2 million that we expended, so we are still carrying a debt from that. We spent $2 million on registration, and quite a bit on polling for our congressional, senatorial, and gubernatorial candidates. Another major role that the Democratic National Committee played was to be a complaint bureau for all our state chairmen, national committee members, and county chairmen. They would call in their grievances; and I don't know if Bob Keefe or Bob Strauss or I could do anything about them, but at least we listened and gave people a chance to vent.

CRITICAL FACTORS IN CARTER WIN

OTTEN: Looking back in general, what were the three or four critical factors that made Governor Carter the winner and allowed President Ford to come as close as he did, considering all the handicaps he was under?

CADDELL: The Ford campaign was very successful in raising the question of risk versus safety and using it as a negative factor against Carter. But the Carter campaign had a positive factor in the perception of Governor Carter as a new leader who would make the government responsive and concerned about people. A third factor, which was not so great a factor as it could have been, was the use of the economic issues, particularly as unemployment began to surpass inflation as a concern. There were many other factors—like voter registration—that contributed to the Carter victory. But it was particularly important that early on the Carter campaign focused on

what it really needed, which was to hold the South, hold those traditionally Democratic states that we counted as the base, and hold at
least the two states in which we had won major primary victories and
already invested a lot of money—Ohio and Pennsylvania. That early
baseline strategy worked all the way through.

TEETER: Given the fact that Governor Carter had the Southern
base and probably the traditional Democratic states, the Ford campaign was in the position of having to draw to an inside straight elec-
torally in order to get 270 electoral votes—and we missed by two
states, Ohio and Wisconsin. We just never had a chance to get out
from under that problem. On the positive side, the Vail meeting was
a great boost for the Ford campaign, marking a change in the president's attitude toward and understanding of the campaign. The decision that Ford ought to be perceived as president and stay in the
White House a great deal prevented a lot of mistakes that had been
made previously. A most important positive factor for the Ford campaign was our advertising. But a final negative factor: the mistake in
the second debate was very, very important. When you have a margin
of one or two points in an election, anything that was worth a point
or two was the crucial thing.

DUVAL: In trying to plan the strategy for the Ford campaign, we
worked out the likely sequence of actions and reactions on both
sides. Our analysis was surprisingly close to what actually happened,
but there were a couple of instances where we had hoped they would
react and they didn't. For instance, they did not react to the anti-
Carter advertising with anti-Ford advertising. We all hoped that they
would attack the president in advertising, but their discipline held.

DEARDOURFF: In talking about political campaigns, you have to
realize that the events of the real world are as important as the crea-
tive events of the campaign. One fact of the real world was that the
president was a Republican who had been associated very closely
with Nixon, particularly with the pardon, and the Ford campaign
never overcame the damage done by that fact. Another fact of the
real world was that the economy went flat, and at some point unemployment surpassed inflation as the major concern of voters. This
hurt us very badly. We were also hurt by the second debate which
underlined the competence question that we had tried so hard to
overcome. I think we were also hurt by the president as a status quo
president.

CHARLES S. SNIDER (campaign director for Wallace): There was one absolutely obvious fact about the campaign: that it would be decided in the South, and that the Ford people were writing off the South. It was just unbelievable to me that the necessary steps weren't taken to bring Ronald Reagan into the South, even if people had to swallow their pride and beg him to come. I was expecting any day to see Ronald Reagan traveling around the South with about half of our supporters. It would have made a big difference in the final outcome.

NOFZIGER: We Reagan people are probably overly sensitive, but we thought that it was a mistake not to invite Reagan and Reagan's leadership to Vail, to try to make us a part of the overall Republican effort from the beginning. I don't believe that any such attempt was ever really made; whatever overtures there eventually were came so late that many Reagan people felt they had to fight their way in or they were being relegated to lesser positions or they were being left out.

TEETER: It was a mistake not to invite Reagan to Vail. At the same time, when he ultimately did campaign for Ford in Texas, you couldn't say he overdid his praise of the president. Essentially, he was campaigning for the platform; he spent two days in Texas and mentioned the president about once a day.

IMPACT OF CAMPAIGN FINANCE LAW

OTTEN: What impact did the campaign finance law have on the campaign?

KEENE: Some people said at the time the statute was drafted that it tended to help incumbents, at the presidential level and at lower levels. Not only was it a proincumbent act, it was essentially an anti-grassroots act. It shut off a lot of things that people used to do, and in that way was detrimental to the whole political system. It tended to emphasize media because you had some money and you couldn't give it to people for grassroots activity.

KEEFE: It wasn't just that you couldn't afford bumperstickers or that sort of thing; it was that campaign managers found themselves actively discouraging people from doing things which would have been considered contributions in kind or which would have put the campaign over its limit. There was actual discouragement of activity by people who really wanted to do it, and they didn't understand it.

JOHN M. QUINN (campaign director for Udall): What was trouble-some to the Udall campaign was the constant uncertainty of the cash flow. Even after a submission was made, we never knew when the money would be coming back. This made planning impossible be-cause you didn't even know what primary you could use the money in.

RAFSHOON: From my standpoint, all these things took too much time away from thinking about the campaign as a political operation. I was constantly thinking first about the law, all the financial arrange-ments around it, the recording problems, the timetables, and the money flow, and I really had a hell of a time concentrating on trying to do my job.

JAMES M. FRIEDMAN (campaign manager for Bayh): When you're building with contributions of $1,000 each, time becomes a vital fac-tor, particularly in the primary process. It is impossible, physically and otherwise, to raise several million dollars within a year before the first primary.

JESSICA TUCHMAN (director of issues and research for Udall): Pos-sibly one of the big lessons of 1976 is going to be that two year cam-paigns are now obligatory. I think that is potentially very negative in that it may limit the nomination to those men and women who are single-minded enough to dedicate two and a half years of full-time work to this pursuit. It seems impossible for anybody with heavy congressional obligations or for a governor in office to undertake the kind of campaign necessary the year before the calendar year of the election. This has an enormous effect on who can even try for the presidency.

MOE: There are some changes that should be made in the law, but I think the law worked extremely well in terms of what Congress in-tended it to accomplish originally. The law permitted a candidate to come from nowhere and to raise enough money to be nominated and eventually elected without being encumbered by large obligations. It's the first time in history that this has happened. The primary financing worked particularly well because it was tied to the candi-dates' popular and political support. In the general election, I have some problems with the block grant in that it prohibits the partici-pation of people who want to participate by contributing money. But it was the first time that spending was equalized—which clearly worked to the Democrats' advantage. All in all, the law did what Congress had in mind when it enacted it.

DUVAL: I've heard talk about requiring debates as a condition for federal money, and other similar kinds of things. In my opinion, there's far too much statutory and regulatory interference in the presidential election as it is; if people are thinking of adding more, I think they're wrong.

KEENE: At the very least, I think there has to be an increase in the individual contribution limit at the presidential level. Given the limit that exists and the amount of time available, a candidate who is trying to get started simply cannot raise the money necessary to run a viable campaign. And the great growth in the number of primaries has compounded the problem. I also think that the total amount of money that can be spent should be freed up; the limits are too low. One of the problems with regulation is that every time you free anything from regulation, you're creating what proponents of regulation like to call a loophole. But the people out there in the country who want to be involved in politics ought to be able to be involved, even if you have to create a loophole to let them be. The objective of cleaning up the system was a decent goal, a goal that we should all be interested in. But I don't think that much of what was incorporated in the new law was necessary to accomplish that goal. I think the law ought to be looked at very critically.

KEEFE: I think the campaign law was drafted largely by people with experience only in congressional races and so forth; as they rework the law, they ought to consult with people who have experience in presidential campaigns.

CADDELL: There's no doubt that in 1976 the Democrats gained an advantage from there being enforced equal funding. But there seems to be a consensus that the overall expenditure allowed was not enough, mostly because of the limiting effects on grassroots activity.

OTTEN: But if the expenditure limit were raised, would the money be used at the grassroots? Wouldn't the tendency be to pump more millions into the media, because a presidential candidate is less concerned about the viability of the party than about the viability of the candidate?

DEARDOURFF: The Ford campaign could not have spent more on media. In fact, at the very end of the campaign, the organizational people were actually giving money back to us. Faced with all the confining regulations, they hadn't been able to go out and organize themselves in a way that would allow them to spend the money. We spent $12 million on media in two months, and we didn't want to spend more. The additional money should have been used effectively in encouraging, promoting, and stimulating grassroots political activity.

MOE: But even beyond the new laws, I think that you can make a very strong case that the whole nominating process is a very irrational process. There is no constitutional basis for it; it's a jumble of factors coming together—partly custom, partly state law, partly party regulation, partly federal law. A year or so ago, Senator Mondale tried to set up a commission to look at the whole process comprehensively and thoroughly, but unfortunately, [Ohio Congressman] Wayne Hays took that with him when he left Congress. There are things that might bring some rationality to this process—a regional primary system would be my preference, and others have suggested a national primary. The problem is that nobody has ever taken a comprehensive look at the nominating process, and it's badly in need of review.

IMPORTANCE OF ISSUES

OTTEN: On the basis of the experience of the 1976 campaign, would you expect issues to decrease in importance in the future, except insofar as they may relate to a candidate's leadership qualities?

BEN J. WATTENBERG (adviser to Jackson): Both Carter and Ford stressed that the real operative issue in this election was the question of "traditional American values." I would argue that this was truly an issue, or issue cluster, not a matter of personalities. It had aspects of economics and foreign policy both in the primaries and in the general election. Four years ago, people debated whether this was a traditionalist country or whether it was a country in the midst of great change, as represented by the various cause movements of the 1960s. That question has been answered in the most obvious of political ways—when both candidates take the same position, you know that means something.

KEENE: We can talk about personality or "traditional American values" or whatever, but the fact is that voters are both selecting leaders and concerning themselves with issues. This year there was some confusion about how to judge the candidates, because of the 1972 experience and Watergate and things of that sort; but I would maintain that in recent years, in general, voters have tended to be more and more concerned with issues. By and large, the people involved in the Reagan campaign did not have a great professional or organizational stake in the outcome of the race; they were involved because they cared about the candidate and about the issues he stood for. Regardless of how the factors in a campaign may be manipulated, the people who are making decisions among the candidates at both the primary and general election level oftentimes are making them on issues, at least as broadly understood. This is something that isn't going to change, and should be maximized to the extent that it can be.

DEARDOURFF: It seems to me that the reaction to the 1972 campaign was a part of the strategic thinking of both camps as they came up to 1976. In 1972 Nixon had won largely because voters believed that he was correct on issues or because they found McGovern's position on issues unacceptable. Then it was suddenly revealed that Nixon had incredible character flaws, and the fact that he was correct on issues had no meaning. As we began to think about 1976, our great concern was that we present the president as a man who could be trusted, who was innately a man of integrity, who was all of the things that Nixon was not. Issues became part of our effort to persuade people that Ford was right from a human point of view. But I think the overwhelming mass of American voters is not preoccupied with issues. The intellectual community and the working press are sophisticated and knowledgeable and interested in the substance of issues, but the average voter, whose information is communicated almost entirely by electronic means, is interested only in the broad sweep of issues—whether you're strong or weak on foreign policy, whether you're for more or less government, for tax cuts or tax increases. Voters simply are not, in my judgment, either interested enough or well enough educated to perceive the complexities. Our job as campaign professionals is to try to reach voters with messages that are appealing to them, not to try to communicate more than they are willing or able to absorb.

FRIEDMAN: All of us here are involved almost full time in campaign decisions. We think about them with an intensity unknown to voters, and we tend to overemphasize the aggregate effect that a campaign has on the number of votes counted on each side. No two year campaign could rationally try to change the views of enough people in the electorate to change the outcome of an election. No campaign is going to change the way twenty million people think about the economy—whether they think inflation or unemployment is more important. What a campaign can do is to affect whether or not voters believe a candidate is compatible with what they already think.

CADDELL: Deciding on a candidate's character is an important judgment for people to make, and in a presidential election, it's a complicated one. Beyond this, I find that voters are not simplistic in their views about issues—in fact, they've gained a greater understanding of the complexity of problems. But we've seen a devaluation of issues because people no longer believe that the government is going to solve problems or that there are rational solutions that are going to be implemented, in the area of crime or the economy or whatever. What we're looking at is not a failure of the political process, but a failure of the governmental process. As a result of that failure, politics has become a spectator sport for some people: the value judgments that they make in voting are affected by their expectation that none of it makes any difference. As long as that's the operating premise on the part of the public, you're not going to have issue-oriented elections; and that's a problem that can be solved only on the governmental level, not in the political process.

TEETER: The movement toward candidate rather than issue voting occurred in the middle to late 1960s and then was amplified by Watergate. One of the basic reasons for it was that voters were concerned about the difficulty of deciding between two candidates in any given election on the basis of a large number of very complex issues. So they began to look for someone who seemed best qualified to handle a large number of complex issues. I think a large number of voters have decided that what we ought to do when thinking about presidential candidates is to find the most trustworthy, competent individual, and not try to sort things out on the basis of three or four or a dozen issues. When we talk about voters' perceptions of candidates, we are not referring to speaking ability, what kind of clothes a candidate wears, or how attractive a personality a candidate has; we're talking about perceptions of intelligence, trustworthiness, judgment, and the kind of temperament it takes to hold an important public office. Such personal perceptions are legitimate and very important. At this point, I tend to agree with the wisdom of a large number of American voters, rather than a few people in the press and the academic community who persist in saying that it is a bad thing that we are not considering issues. When you think of the job of president, and how long a president is in office, it is hard to say that the important issues any president will deal with will be the ones debated in a campaign. Who knows what important decisions Jimmy Carter is going to have to make in the next four years? None of us could possibly imagine, and I think a large number of voters have come to understand that.

Appendixes

Appendix A

Some Campaign Dates

1974

August 9	Vice President Gerald R. Ford was sworn in as thirty-eighth president.
September 8	President Ford granted a pardon to former President Richard M. Nixon.
September 23	Senator Edward M. Kennedy (Democrat, Massachusetts) announced that he would not be a candidate for president in 1976.
November 21	Senator Walter F. Mondale (Democrat, Minnesota) announced that he would not seek the Democratic presidential nomination.
November 23	Congressman Morris K. Udall (Democrat, Arizona) declared that he would try for the Democratic nomination.
December 7	A midterm convention of the Democratic party was held in Kansas City, and a party charter was adopted.
December 12	Former Governor Jimmy Carter of Georgia announced that he would seek the Democratic presidential nomination by entering all the state primaries and gathering delegates in the non-primary state caucuses and conventions.
December 19	Former Governor Nelson A. Rockefeller of New York was sworn in as vice president.

1975

January 11	Former Senator Fred R. Harris (Democrat, Oklahoma) announced his candidacy for the Democratic presidential nomination.
January 12	Former Senator Eugene J. McCarthy (Democrat, Minnesota) said that he would be an independent candidate for president in 1976.
February 6	Senator Henry M. Jackson (Democrat, Washington) announced that he would seek the Democratic presidential nomination.
February 17	Senator Lloyd M. Bentsen (Democrat, Texas) became the fifth declared candidate for the Democratic nomination.
May 29	Former North Carolina Governor Terry Sanford entered the Democratic race.
July 8	President Ford formally announced that he would be a candidate for the Republican nomination.
September 20	Former Ambassador R. Sargent Shriver, Jr., declared his candidacy for the Democratic nomination.
September 25	Governor Milton J. Shapp of Pennsylvania entered the Democratic race, becoming the eighth candidate to declare.
October 21	Senator Birch Bayh (Democrat, Indiana) announced that he would seek the Democratic presidential nomination.
November 3	In a letter to President Ford, Vice President Rockefeller said that he did not want to be a candidate for vice president in the 1976 race.
November 12	Governor George C. Wallace of Alabama entered the race for the Democratic nomination.
November 20	Former Governor Ronald Reagan of California announced that he would challenge President Ford for the Republican presidential nomination.
December 6	The convention of the New York New Democratic Coalition was held in New York City.

1976

January 2	The Federal Election Commission began distributing campaign money to the eleven candidates who had qualified for the federal funds.
January 9	Senator Robert C. Byrd (Democrat, West Virginia) announced his candidacy for the Democratic presidential nomination.

January 19	Iowa Democrats held their precinct caucuses for selection of convention delegates and thus provided the first test of strength for the Democratic presidential candidates (see Appendix B for results of 1976 delegate selection caucuses).
January 23	Governor Sanford withdrew from the Democratic race.
January 30	The Supreme Court handed down its decision interpreting the 1974 Federal Election Campaign Act and striking down some of its provisions.
February 10	Senator Bentsen withdrew from the Democratic race.
February 24	New Hampshire opened the presidential preference primary season (see Appendix B for 1976 primary vote totals and percentages).
March 2	Massachusetts primary.
	Vermont primary.
March 4	Senator Bayh suspended his active campaign for the Democratic presidential nomination.
March 9	Florida primary.
March 12	Governor Edmund G. Brown, Jr., of California announced that he would enter the California primary in June as a candidate for the Democratic nomination.
	Governor Shapp withdrew from the Democratic race.
March 16	Illinois primary.
March 18	Senator Frank Church (Democrat, Idaho) entered the Democratic race.
March 22	The Federal Election Commission temporarily stopped disbursing federal funds.
	Ambassador Shriver withdrew from the Democratic race.
March 23	North Carolina primary.
March 30	Howard H. Callaway resigned as President Ford's campaign manager and was replaced by Rogers C.B. Morton.
April 6	New York primary (delegate selection only).
	Wisconsin primary.
April 8	Senator Harris suspended his active campaign effort.
April 27	Pennsylvania primary.
April 29	Senator Hubert H. Humphrey (Democrat, Minnesota) announced that he would not actively seek the Democratic presidential nomination.

May 1	Senator Jackson suspended his campaign.
	Texas primary (delegate selection only).
May 3	Senator Bayh endorsed Governor Carter for the Democratic nomination.
May 4	Alabama primary (delegate selection only).
	District of Columbia primary.
	Georgia primary.
	Indiana primary.
May 11	Nebraska primary.
	West Virginia primary.
May 18	Maryland primary.
	Michigan primary.
May 21	The Federal Election Commission resumed its functions, distributing federal funds.
May 25	Arkansas primary.
	Idano primary.
	Kentucky primary.
	Nevada primary.
	Oregon primary.
	Tennessee primary.
June 1	Montana primary.
	Rhode Island primary.
	South Dakota primary.
June 8	California primary.
	New Jersey primary.
	Ohio primary.
June 9	Governor Carter was endorsed by Governor Wallace and by Mayor Richard J. Daley of Chicago.
June 14	Senator Church withdrew from the race and endorsed Governor Carter; Congressman Udall suspended his campaign but did not withdraw.
June 15	It was announced that Governor Carter officially had the 1,505 delegates needed for the Democratic nomination.

June 17   Senator Jackson endorsed Governor Carter.

July 14   Meeting in New York City, the Democratic convention nomi-
                 nated Governor Carter for president and Senator Mondale
                 for vice president.

July 26   Governor Reagan announced that Senator Richard S. Schwei-
                 ker of Pennsylvania would be his vice presidential running
                 mate if he were to win the Republican presidential nomination.

August 16   Meeting in Kansas City, the Republican convention began its
                 proceedings and subsequently nominated President Ford for
                 president and Senator Robert J. Dole of Kansas for vice
                 president.

August 25   James A. Baker, III, became the third chairman of the Presi-
                 dent Ford Committee, replacing Rogers C.B. Morton.

September 6   Labor Day: the general election campaign officially began.

September 23   The first of the televised debates between President Ford and
                 Governor Carter was held in Philadelphia, concerning domes-
                 tic issues.

October 7   The second televised Ford-Carter debate was held in San
                 Francisco, concerning foreign policy issues.

October 15   A debate between vice presidential candidates Dole and Mon-
                 dale was televised from Houston.

October 22   The third televised debate between President Ford and Gov-
                 ernor Carter was held in Williamsburg, Virginia.

November 2   Election Day: Governor Carter won the presidency with a
                 popular vote of 51 percent over President Ford's 48 percent,
                 and an electoral vote of 297 to 240. Independent candidate
                 McCarthy received about 1 percent of the popular vote.

Appendix B

Some Campaign Statistics

1976 CONVENTION DELEGATES FROM STATES HOLDING DELEGATE SELECTION CAUCUSES, CONVENTIONS, AND PRIMARIES

State	Republican				Democratic													
	Ford	Reagan	Uncommitted	Total	Bayh	Bentsen	Brown	Carter	Church	Harris	Jackson	Humphrey	McCormack	Shriver	Udall	Wallace	Uncommitted	Total
Alabama*		37		37				3								27	5	35
Alaska	17	2		19													10	10
Arizona	2	27		29				5							19	1		25
Colorado	3	26	2	31			6	12	3						5		9	35
Connecticut	35			35				35							16			51
Delaware	13		4	17				10									2	12
Hawaii			19	19							1				1		15	17
Iowa	19	17		36				20		2					12		13	47
Kansas	28	4	2	34				16			1				3		14	34
Louisiana		35	6	41				13								9	19	41
Maine	15	4	1	20				9							5		6	20

State															
Minnesota	33	6	3	42					48					17	65
Mississippi			30	30			5					4	11	4	24
Missouri	16	30	3	49			39		1		1	3		27	71
New Mexico		21		21			9					6		3	18
New York*			154	154			33		103			73		65	274
North Dakota	12	4	2	18			13								13
Oklahoma		36		36			12	7						18	37
South Carolina	1	25	10	36			9	1					8	13	31
Texas*		100		100	6	2	112						1	9	130
Utah		20		20			4	5						9	18
Vermont	17		1	18		2	3					3		4	12
Virginia	6	36	9	51			23					7		24	54
Washington	7	31		38					32			7		14	53
Wyoming			17	17		1	1					1		7	10
TOTAL	224	461	263	948	6	11	386	9	9	138	48	1	4	161	57	307	1137

*Delegate selection primary, with no presidential preference voting.
Source: Delegate figures from *ABC News Factbooks* for the Democratic and Republican conventions.

1976 PRESIDENTIAL PREFERENCE PRIMARIES

The presidential preference primary returns . . . include all candidates who appeared on the ballot in each state and all write-in candidates whose vote totals were reported by the state. Candidate returns in each state are presented in descending order of the number of votes received. . . . Delegate selection primaries were held in Alabama, New York, and Texas. The figures are not recorded here since there was no presidential preference voting.

Republican

February 24 New Hampshire	Votes	%
Gerald R. Ford (Mich.)	55,156	49.4
Ronald Reagan (Calif.)	53,569	48.0
Others[1]	2,949	2.6

March 2 Massachusetts	Votes	%
Ford	115,375	61.2
Reagan	63,555	33.7
None of the names shown	6,000	3.2
Others[1]	3,519	1.8

Democratic

	Votes	%
Jimmy Carter (Ga.)	23,373	28.4
Morris K. Udall (Ariz.)	18,710	22.7
Birch Bayh (Ind.)	12,510	15.2
Fred R. Harris (Okla.)	8,863	10.8
Sargent Shriver (Md.)	6,743	8.2
Hubert H. Humphrey (Minn.)[1]	4,596	5.6
Henry M. Jackson (Wash.)[1]	1,857	2.3
George C. Wallace (Ala.)[1]	1,061	1.3
Ellen McCormack (N.Y.)	1,007	1.2
Others	3,661	4.8

	Votes	%
Jackson	164,393	22.3
Udall	130,440	17.7
Wallace	123,112	16.7
Carter	101,948	13.9
Harris	55,701	7.6

Shriver	53,252	7.2
Bayh	34,963	4.8
McCormack	25,772	3.5
Milton J. Shapp (Pa.)	21,693	2.9
None of the names shown	9,804	1.3
Humphrey[1]	7,851	1.1
Edward M. Kennedy (Mass.)[1]	1,623	0.2
Lloyd Bentsen (Texas)	364	—
Others	4,905	0.7

March 2   Vermont

Ford	27,014	84.0
Reagan[1]	4,892	15.2
Others[1]	251	—

Carter	16,335	42.2
Shriver	10,699	27.6
Harris	4,893	12.6
McCormack	3,324	8.6
Others	3,463	9.0

March 9   Florida

Ford	321,982	52.8
Reagan	287,837	47.2

Carter	448,844	34.5
Wallace	396,820	30.5
Jackson	310,944	23.9
None of the names shown	37,626	2.9
Shapp	32,198	2.5
Udall	27,235	2.1
Bayh	8,750	0.7
McCormack	7,595	0.6
Shriver	7,084	0.5
Harris	5,397	0.4
Robert C. Byrd (W. Va.)	5,042	0.4
Frank Church (Idaho)	4,906	0.4
Others	7,889	0.6

Republican

March 16   Illinois

	Votes	%
Ford	456,750	58.9
Reagan	311,295	40.1
Lar Daly (Ill.)	7,582	1.0
Others[1]	266	—

March 23   North Carolina

	Votes	%
Reagan	101,468	52.4
Ford	88,897	45.9
None of the names shown	3,362	1.7

April 6   Wisconsin

	Votes	%
Ford	326,869	55.2
Reagan	262,126	44.3
None of the names shown	2,234	0.3
Others[1]	583	—

Democratic

Illinois

	Votes	%
Carter	630,915	48.1
Wallace	361,798	27.6
Shriver	214,024	16.3
Harris	98,862	7.5
Others[1]	6,315	0.5

North Carolina

	Votes	%
Carter	324,437	53.6
Wallace	210,166	34.7
Jackson	25,749	4.3
None of the names shown	22,850	3.8
Udall	14,032	2.3
Harris	5,923	1.0
Bentsen	1,675	0.3

Wisconsin

	Votes	%
Carter	271,220	36.6
Udall	263,771	35.6
Wallace	92,460	12.5
Jackson	47,605	6.4
McCormack	26,982	3.6
Harris	8,185	1.1
None of the names shown	7,154	1.0
Shriver	5,097	0.7
Bentsen	1,730	0.2
Bayh	1,255	0.2
Shapp	596	0.1
Others[1]	14,473	2.0

April 27 — Pennsylvania

Ford	733,472	92.1
Reagan[1]	40,510	5.1
Others[1]	22,678	2.8
Carter	511,905	37.0
Jackson	340,340	24.6
Udall	259,166	18.7
Wallace	155,902	11.3
McCormack	38,800	2.8
Shapp	32,947	2.4
Bayh	15,320	1.1
Harris	13,067	0.9
Humphrey[1]	12,563	0.9
Others	5,032	0.3

May 4 — District of Columbia

[2]

Carter	10,521	31.6
Walter E. Fauntroy (unpledged delegates)	10,149	30.5
Udall	6,999	21.0
Walter E. Washington (unpledged delegates)	5,161	15.5
Harris	461	1.4

May 4 — Georgia

Reagan	128,671	68.3
Ford	59,801	31.7
Carter	419,272	83.4
Wallace	57,594	11.5
Udall	9,755	1.9
Byrd	3,628	0.7
Jackson	3,358	0.7
Church	2,477	0.5
Shriver	1,378	0.3
Bayh	824	0.2
Harris	699	0.1
McCormack	635	0.1
Bentsen	277	0.1
Shapp	181	—
Others	2,393	0.5

Republican

May 4 — Indiana

	Votes	%
Reagan	323,779	51.3
Ford	307,513	48.7

May 11 — Nebraska

	Votes	%
Reagan	113,493	54.5
Ford	94,542	45.4
Others	379	0.1

May 11 — West Virginia

	Votes	%
Ford	88,386	56.8
Reagan	67,306	43.2

Democratic

Indiana

	Votes	%
Carter	417,480	68.0
Wallace	93,121	15.2
Jackson	72,080	11.7
McCormack	31,708	5.2

Nebraska

	Votes	%
Church	67,297	38.5
Carter	65,833	37.6
Humphrey	12,685	7.2
Kennedy	7,199	4.1
McCormack	6,033	3.4
Wallace	5,567	3.2
Udall	4,688	2.7
Jackson	2,642	1.5
Harris	811	0.5
Bayh	407	0.2
Shriver	384	0.2
Others	1,467	0.8

West Virginia

	Votes	%
Byrd	331,639	89.0
Wallace	40,938	11.0

May 18   Maryland

Ford	96,291	58.0	Edmund G. Brown Jr. (Calif.)	286,672	48.4
Reagan	69,680	42.0	Carter	219,404	37.1
			Udall	32,790	5.5
			Wallace	24,176	4.1
			Jackson	13,956	2.4
			McCormack	7,907	1.3
			Harris	6,841	1.2

May 18   Michigan

Ford	690,180	64.9	Carter	307,559	43.4
Reagan	364,052	34.3	Udall	305,134	43.1
Unpledged delegates	8,473	0.8	Wallace	49,204	6.9
Others[1]	109	—	Unpledged delegates	15,853	2.2
			Jackson	10,332	1.5
			McCormack	7,623	1.1
			Shriver	5,738	0.8
			Harris	4,081	0.6
			Others[1]	3,142	0.4

May 25   Arkansas

Reagan	20,628	63.4	Carter	314,306	62.6
Ford	11,430	35.1	Wallace	83,005	16.5
Unpledged delegates	483	1.5	Unpledged delegates	57,152	11.4
			Udall	37,783	7.5
			Jackson	9,554	1.9

Republican

Idaho

May 25

	Votes	%
Reagan	66,743	74.3
Ford	22,323	24.9
Unpledged delegates	727	0.8

Kentucky

May 25

	Votes	%
Ford	67,976	50.9
Reagan	62,683	46.9
Unpledged delegates	1,781	1.3
Others	1,088	0.8

Nevada

May 25

	Votes	%
Reagan	31,637	66.3
Ford	13,747	28.8
None of the names shown	2,365	5.0

Democratic

Idaho

	Votes	%
Church	58,570	78.7
Carter	8,818	11.9
Humphrey	1,700	2.3
Brown[1]	1,453	2.0
Wallace	1,115	1.5
Udall	981	1.3
Unpledged delegates	964	1.3
Jackson	485	0.7
Harris	319	0.4

Kentucky

	Votes	%
Carter	181,690	59.4
Wallace	51,540	16.8
Udall	33,262	10.9
McCormack	17,061	5.6
Unpledged delegates	11,962	3.9
Jackson	8,186	2.7
Others	2,305	0.8

Nevada

	Votes	%
Brown	39,671	52.7
Carter	17,567	23.3
Church	6,778	9.0
None of the names shown	4,603	6.1
Wallace	2,490	3.3
Udall	2,237	3.0
Jackson	1,896	2.5

May 25   *Oregon*

Ford	150,181	50.3
Reagan	136,691	45.8
Others[1]	11,663	3.9

Church	145,394	33.6
Carter	115,310	26.7
Brown[1]	106,812	24.7
Humphrey	22,488	5.2
Udall	11,747	2.7
Kennedy	10,983	2.5
Wallace	5,797	1.3
Jackson	5,298	1.2
McCormack	3,753	0.9
Harris	1,344	0.3
Bayh	743	0.2
Others[1]	2,963	0.7

May 25   *Tennessee*

Ford	120,685	49.8
Reagan	118,997	49.1
Unpledged delegates	2,756	1.1
Others[1]	97	—

Carter	259,243	77.6
Wallace	36,495	10.9
Udall	12,420	3.7
Church	8,026	2.4
Unpledged delegates	6,148	1.8
Jackson	5,672	1.7
McCormack	1,782	0.5
Harris	1,628	0.5
Brown[1]	1,556	0.5
Shapp	507	0.2
Humphrey[1]	109	—
Others[1]	492	0.1

Republican

June 1   Montana

	Votes	%
Reagan	56,683	63.1
Ford	31,100	34.6
None of the names shown	1,996	2.2

June 1   Rhode Island

	Votes	%
Ford	9,365	65.3
Reagan	4,480	31.2
Unpledged delegates	507	3.5

June 1   South Dakota

	Votes	%
Reagan	43,068	51.2
Ford	36,976	44.0
None of the names shown	4,033	4.8

Democratic

Montana

	Votes	%
Church	63,448	59.4
Carter	26,329	24.6
Udall	6,708	6.3
None of the names shown	3,820	3.6
Wallace	3,680	3.4
Jackson	2,856	2.7

Rhode Island

	Votes	%
Unpledged delegates	19,035	31.5
Carter	18,237	30.2
Church	16,423	27.2
Udall	2,543	4.2
McCormack	2,468	4.1
Jackson	756	1.3
Wallace	507	0.8
Bayh	247	0.4
Shapp	132	0.2

South Dakota

	Votes	%
Carter	24,186	41.2
Udall	19,510	33.3
None of the names shown	7,871	13.4
McCormack	4,561	7.8
Wallace	1,412	2.4
Harris	573	1.0
Jackson	558	1.0

June 8 **California**

Reagan	1,604,836	65.5
Ford	845,655	34.5
Others[1]	20	—
Brown	2,013,210	59.0
Carter	697,092	20.4
Church	250,581	7.3
Udall	171,501	5.0
Wallace	102,292	3.0
Unpledged delegates	78,595	2.3
Jackson	38,634	1.1
McCormack	29,242	0.9
Harris	16,920	0.5
Bayh	11,419	0.3
Others[1]	215	—

June 8 **New Jersey**

Ford	242,122	100.0
Carter	210,655	58.4
Church	49,034	13.6
Jackson	31,820	8.8
Wallace	31,183	8.6
McCormack	21,774	6.0
Others	16,373	4.5

June 8 **Ohio**

Ford	516,111	55.2
Reagan	419,646	44.8
Carter	593,130	52.3
Udall	240,342	21.2
Church	157,884	13.9
Wallace	63,953	5.6
Gertrude W. Donahey (unpledged delegates)	43,661	3.9
Jackson	35,404	3.1

Republican

TOTALS	Votes	%
Ford	5,529,899	53.3
Reagan	4,758,325	45.9
None of the names shown	19,990	0.2
Unpledged delegates	14,727	0.1
Daly	7,582	0.1
Others[3]	43,602	0.4
	10,374,125	

Democratic

	Votes	%
Carter	6,235,609	38.8
Brown	2,449,374	15.3
Wallace	1,995,388	12.4
Udall	1,611,754	10.0
Jackson	1,134,375	7.1
Church	830,818	5.2
Byrd	340,309	2.1
Shriver	304,399	1.9
Unpledged delegates	248,680	1.5
McCormack	238,027	1.5
Harris	234,568	1.5
None of the names shown	93,728	0.6
Shapp	88,254	0.5
Bayh	86,438	0.5
Humphrey	61,992	0.4
Kennedy	19,905	0.1
Bentsen	4,046	—
Others[4]	75,088	0.5
	16,052,652	

1. Write-in.

2. Ford unopposed. No primary held.

3. In addition to scattered write-in votes, "others" include Tommy Klein, who received 1,088 votes in Kentucky.

4. In addition to scattered write-in votes, "others" include Frank Ahern who received 1,487 votes in Georgia; Stanley Arnold, 371 votes in New Hampshire; Arthur O. Blessitt, 828 votes in New Hampshire and 7,889 in Georgia; Frank Bona, 135 votes in New Hampshire and 263 in Georgia; Billy Joe Clegg, 174 votes in New Hampshire; Abram Eisenman, 351 votes in Georgia; John S. Gonas, 2,288 votes in New Jersey; Jesse Gray, 3,571 votes in New Jersey; Robert L. Kelleher, 87 votes in New Hampshire, 1,603 in Massachusetts and 139 in Georgia; Rick Loewenherz, 49 votes in New Hampshire; Frank Lomento, 3,555 votes in New Jersey; Floyd L. Lunger, 3,935 votes in New Jersey; H.R.H. "Fifi" Rockefeller, 2,305 votes in Kentucky; George Roden, 153 votes in Georgia; Ray Rollinson, 3,021 votes in New Jersey; Terry Sanford, 53 votes in New Hampshire and 351 votes in Massachusetts; Bernard B. Schechter, 173 votes in New Hampshire.

Source: *Congressional Quarterly*, editorial research report.

PRESIDENTIAL ELECTION STATISTICS

Popular and Electoral Vote, 1972 and 1976

States	*1972*			
	Electoral Vote		*Popular Vote*	
	Nixon	*McGovern*	*Nixon*	*McGovern*
Alabama	9		728,701	256,923
Alaska	3		55,349	32,967
Arizona	6		402,812	198,540
Arkansas	6		445,751	198,899
California	45		4,602,096	3,475,847
Colorado	7		597,189	329,980
Connecticut	8		810,763	555,498
Delaware	3		140,357	92,298
District of Columbia		3	35,226	127,627
Florida	17		1,857,759	718,117
Georgia	12		881,496	289,529
Hawaii	4		168,865	101,409
Idaho	4		199,384	80,826
Illinois	26		2,788,179	1,913,472
Indiana	13		1,405,154	708,568
Iowa	8		706,207	496,206
Kansas	7		619,812	270,287
Kentucky	9		676,446	371,159
Louisiana	10		686,852	298,142
Maine	4		256,458	160,584
Maryland	10		829,305	505,781
Massachusetts		14	1,112,078	1,332,540
Michigan	21		1,961,721	1,459,435
Minnesota	10		898,269	802,346
Mississippi	7		505,125	126,872
Missouri	12		1,154,058	698,531
Montana	4		183,976	120,197
Nebraska	5		406,298	169,991
Nevada	3		115,750	66,016
New Hampshire	4		213,724	116,435
New Jersey	17		1,845,502	1,102,211
New Mexico	4		235,606	141,084
New York	41		4,192,778	2,951,084
North Carolina	13		1,054,889	438,705
North Dakota	3		174,109	100,384
Ohio	25		2,441,827	1,558,889
Oklahoma	8		759,025	247,147
Oregon	6		486,686	392,760
Pennsylvania	27		2,714,521	1,796,951
Rhode Island	4		218,290	191,981

Popular and Electoral Vote, 1972 and 1976 (cont'd.)

	1976			
Electoral Vote		*Popular Vote*		
Carter	*Ford*	*Carter*	*Ford*	*McCarthy*
9		659,170	504,070	
	3	44,058	71,555	
	6	295,602	418,642	19,229
6		498,604	267,903	639
	45	3,742,284	3,882,244	
	7	460,801	584,278	26,047
	8	347,895	719,261	
3		122,461	109,780	2,432
3		137,818	27,873	
17		1,636,000	1,469,531	23,643
12		979,409	483,743	
4		147,375	140,003	
	4	126,549	204,151	
	26	2,271,295	2,364,269	55,939
	13	1,014,714	1,185,958	
	8	619,931	632,863	20,051
	7	430,421	502,752	13,185
9		615,717	531,852	6,837
10		661,365	587,446	6,490
	4	232,279	236,320	10,874
10		759,612	672,661	
14		1,429,475	1,030,276	65,637
	21	1,696,714	1,893,742	47,905
10		1,070,440	819,395	35,490
7		381,329	366,846	4,074
12		998,387	927,443	24,029
	4	149,259	173,703	
	5	233,293	359,219	9,383
	3	92,479	101,273	
	4	147,645	185,935	4,095
	17	1,444,653	1,509,688	32,717
	4	201,148	211,419	
41		3,389,558	3,100,791	
13		927,365	741,960	
	3	136,078	153,684	2,952
25		2,009,959	2,000,626	58,267
	8	532,442	545,708	14,101
	6	490,407	492,120	40,207
27		2,328,677	2,205,604	50,584
4		227,636	181,249	

(continued on pages 184 & 185)

Popular and Electoral Vote, 1972 and 1976 (cont'd.)

	1972			
States	*Electoral Vote*		*Popular Vote*	
	Nixon	*McGovern*	*Nixon*	*McGovern*
South Carolina	8		477,044	186,824
South Dakota	4		166,476	139,945
Tennessee	10		813,147	357,293
Texas	26		2,298,896	1,154,289
Utah	4		323,643	126,284
Vermont	3		117,149	68,174
Virginia	11*		988,493	438,887
Washington	9		837,135	568,334
West Virginia	6		484,964	277,435
Wisconsin	11		989,430	810,174
Wyoming	3		100,464	44,358
TOTAL	520	17	47,165,234	28,168,110

*One elector in Virginia for John Hospers and Theodora Nathan
**One elector in Washington for Ronald Reagan
Source: *The World Almanac and Book of Facts*, 1978 edition:
        copyright © Newspaper Enterprise Association, 1977.

Popular and Electoral Vote, 1972 and 1976 (cont'd.)

1976

Electoral Vote		Popular Vote		
Carter	*Ford*	*Carter*	*Ford*	*McCarthy*
8		450,807	346,149	
	4	147,068	151,505	
10		825,879	633,969	5,004
26		2,082,319	1,953,300	20,118
	4	182,110	337,908	3,907
	3	77,798	100,387	4,001
	12	813,896	836,554	
	8**	717,323	777,732	36,986
6		435,864	314,726	
11		1,040,232	1,004,987	34,943
	3	62,239	92,717	624
297	240	40,825,839	39,147,770	380,390

Index

Abortion, 56, 120
AFL–CIO, 113, 130
Alabama primary: and Ford, 44; and Reagan, 4, 42
American Independent Party, 5
Apple, R.W., 2
Armed Services Committee, 38
Armstrong, Anne, 62

Bailey, Douglas, 65, 136
Baker, James, 59, 60, 62, 123
Bandwagon effect, 36
Barone, Michael, 5
Bayh, Birch: constituency, 77, 83; decision to enter primaries, 77; finances, 76; Florida primary, 95; Iowa caucus, 82, 83–84; and labor, 92, 96; Massachusetts primary, 3; New Democratic Coalition, 77; New Hampshire primary, 91–92; New York primary, 84; primary strategy, 77, 91–92; reelection in Indiana, 76–77; role in campaign plan, 77; and Udall, 77
Bergland, Robert, 100
Black voters, 93–94, 129
Blacks, 102, 105, 114, 139–140
Boston, 2, 13
Brace, Kimball, 5
Brown: California primary, 3; Catholic vote, 108; on issues, 10; late entry, 3, 104; Maryland primary, 3, 100; Nevada primary, 3; *Playboy* inter-

view, 106, 143–144, post-convention campaign, 14; primary strategy, 106–108; on *60 Minutes*, 106
Busing, 13, 89

Caddell, Patrick, 2, 130, 147
California primary: and Brown, 3; and Carter, 3; and Ford, 45; and Reagan, 4, 41, 42, 43, 44–45; "winner take all," 45
Callaway, Bo, 30, 31
Campaign finance law, 33, 43, 151–154
Carter, James Earl: as acceptable alternative to Wallace, 95; advertising in Pennsylvania, 100, and AFL–CIO, 130; "anybody but Carter" movement, 14, 95, 110, 115; anti-Carter advertising, 99–100; as anti-Washington, 46, 87; appeal to middle, 4; blacks involved in campaign, 114; black vote, 129; brokered convention, 81; and Brown, 104; California primary, 3; campaign organization, 129–132; campaign strategy, 124–128; campaign strengths, 118; and Catholic voters, 5, 49, 106, 119; as centrist, 87; and change, 85–86; and Church, 104, 108; critical factors in win, 149–151; and Daley, 109; debates with Ford, 6, 12, 122–123, 126, 139, 141–143; and Democratic National Committee, 148–149; and

187